Zennis

PETER SPANG

Zennis

A PERIGEE BOOK

A Perigee Book
Published by The Berkley Publishing Group
A member of Penguin Putnam Inc.
200 Madison Avenue
New York, NY 10016

First edition: April 1998

Published simultaneously in Canada.

The Penguin Putnam Inc. World Wide Web site address is
http://www.penguinputnam.com

Library of Congress Cataloging-in-Publication Data

Spang, Peter.
    Zennis : an innovative approach to changing your mind, your play,
and your entire tennis experience / Peter Spang. — 1st ed.
        p.   cm.
    "A Perigee book."
    ISBN 0-399-52389-8
    1. Tennis—Psychological aspects.   2. Zen meditations.   I. Title.
GV1002.9.P75S73   1998
796.342—dc21   97-26450
                                                          CIP

10 9 8 7 6 5 4 3 2 1

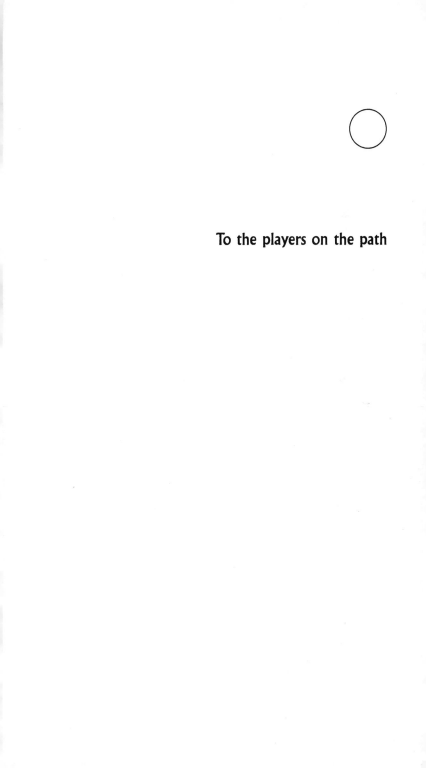

To the players on the path

Contents

Acknowledgments

In writing this book I would like to thank the following people:

Osho, for his courageous vision of combining meditation with love of life. Anando, who first had the idea of a book on Zennis, for being a source of love and inspiration. Subhuti, my ghostwriter and editor, for his ability to ask the right questions, his humor, and his patience. Without him this book would still be an idea. Sheila Curry, for her professionalism in turning the manuscript into a real book.

All my friends who are dedicated to supporting individuals and organizations to create fulfilling futures, like Larry, Andy, Stefan, Mick, Thomas, Gabi, Aja, Micki, Martin, and Vasu.

The Hunger Project and all the people committed to a world free of hunger.

All the players and friends I have met on countless tennis courts, including Axel, Stefan, Gustl, Harald, Sylvia, Stefan Sch., Niki, Damir, Boris, Karina, Horst, Dietmar, Maik, Sepp, Werner, the Augsburg Old Boys, Panthen, KP, Mario, and Torsten Park.

I would also like to thank my parents, Helma and Wolfgang, my brother Michael, and my friends Freya and Andrea.

Introduction

In offering this book I am not trying to bring Zen into tennis. To me, Zen is in tennis already. There is no need to bring it. To experience silent and blissful moments while playing tennis is Zen, and to carry the flavor of these moments into ordinary life is an easy and natural consequence.

Tennis can become a major source of meditative experience for everyone; you don't need to grow a long beard, go to the Himalayas, and sit for years with a guru. In other words, you don't need to change your life to be a meditator.

This book, with all its insights, exercises, and techniques, can help you to make tennis and all sporting activities more vital and enjoyable. It can also help you to relax, go deeper into yourself, and find your own center. In short, this book encourages tennis lovers to become meditators, and meditators to add tennis to their meditations.

At the time when I was a tennis professional, playing every day, practicing for hours, I had no clue how this daily discipline could prepare a person to become a spiritual seeker.

As a professional, you hit the ball so often, you push yourself so hard, you play with such intensity, that sooner or later you are bound to break through into an experience of *the zone*—that mysterious state in which you are playing superbly yet without effort; you are fulfilling your potential, yet without even trying.

Such experiences leave you in a state of awe, and you walk off the tennis court wondering, "What happened today? Am I still on the same planet?" Then, as suddenly as it came, this elusive inner state is gone and you scratch your head and perhaps doubt whether it ever existed.

Such experiences, repeated over time, start you seeking and searching for other ways to arrive at the same state of being. A seed has been planted, and I want to encourage sports lovers to find that seed within themselves, to take the jump into meditation, to become a player on the path of Zen.

What Is It?

A Zen Master was walking with a disciple through a forest one morning when a hare suddenly ran out of a nearby bush and crossed their path.

"What is it?" asked the master.

"A hare," replied the disciple.

The master grabbed the disciple's nose and gave it a fierce twist.

"Ow! You hurt me!" cried the startled disciple.

"It is necessary," replied the master. "Otherwise you will never be able to see what is in front of your nose."

The disciple experienced a sudden insight.

1
Tennis:
A New Way to Watch

"**N**ow Chang is going to break Becker's serve."

"No. I don't think so."

"What odds will you give me?"

"Three to one, Becker holds his serve."

"Okay, you're on."

Michael Chang was playing Boris Becker in the final of the Australian Open. Pete Sampras and Andre Agassi, the two favorites, had been eliminated in earlier rounds. Mark Philippoussis, the great hope of the host nation, had also fallen.

The year was 1996, and I was watching the game live on satellite television with a group of tennis buddies. Phil, a friend of mine, was taking the opportunity to combine his two favorite pastimes, gambling and tennis. He wasn't doing too well, but fortunately for him, the stakes were not $100 Las Vegas chips but tennis balls.

Phil was supporting Chang, and I was favoring Becker. All through the first two sets, my friend was saying, "Now Chang will break Becker's serve," but the German player took these sets in fine style. Even though I was giving Phil generous odds of three to one, each time he bet, my pile of tennis balls kept growing.

Then, at the beginning of the third set, everything changed. Within a very short time, Chang had jumped into a 3–0 lead and was clearly dominating the game. The armchair tennis experts around me quickly reached a consensus:

"Becker is finished now."

"He's tired . . . too old . . . too slow . . . out of shape."

"It's Chang's time now."

I disagreed, not because Becker and I are both German and I was in a patriotic mood, but because I appreciated his performance in the first two sets. He was playing a complex game, mixing it up, not trying to slug it out with Chang from the baseline. This was intelligent because Chang is one of the best counterpunchers in the game. He is fit, fast, and an awesome retriever. You can hit a shot that sends Chang outside the court and he will still reach it and send it back. Against him, the point is never finished.

That's why Agassi had lost to Chang in the semifinals. Playing in the heat and wind, Agassi would hit and hit and hit, but everything he sent over the net would come back to him, until eventually he grew impatient and made mistakes.

Playing Chang, you have to be masterful in your shot selection, which is what Becker had been doing, using short balls to pull Chang out of his natural comfort zone at the baseline, then running to the net himself, executing his own volley game with deadly precision.

When Becker sank to 0–3 in the third set, he suddenly

changed his style of play, making riskier shots, aiming closer to the lines, and consequently making more unforced errors, but I didn't see the tired man that everyone else in the room was seeing. I saw a seasoned competitor trying to conserve his energy at the risk of throwing away a set.

In my view, Becker had deliberately switched to a simple, one-dimensional strategy called *finish the point as soon as possible*. With this strategy, you go for winning shots at the earliest opportunity. You try to hit an ace with every first serve, and if your opponent manages to get the ball back, you hit your next shot so close to the lines that you either hit a winner or the ball is out of play. Even on your second serve, you go for a risky shot.

When your opponent serves and you manage to get your racket on the ball, you immediately try for a dominating return, again by shooting as close to the lines as possible. In this way, no rally goes beyond three points and in this way, too, Becker could avoid exhausting himself by chasing down every ball, engaging in long rallies with the younger, fitter man.

These are all high-risk strategies. Even the best players usually manage only two out of five winners when they play like this, so Becker was making more mistakes and losing points. But his mistakes were only by a few inches—to me, a sure sign that he hadn't lost his precision nor his determination to stay in the game.

In the beginning of the third set, nobody was betting on the game. It was one of those moments when, as a TV spectator, your attention drops because it's time to make coffee or go to the fridge or to the bathroom. When we settled back into watching, Becker was already 0–3 down, and I didn't accept any of Phil's bets until the third set reached a crucial stage in Chang's favor at 5–2.

It was Becker's turn to serve, and if Chang could force a break, he would take the set. I felt that, if I was Becker, I'd want to have this set over and done as soon as possible, conserving my energy for the fourth set. I wouldn't waste time trying to hold my serve game while trailing 5–2 in the Australian summer heat, facing a younger man known to be one of the fittest competitors around.

So, even though I had been betting on Becker, I said to Phil, "Now Chang will break Becker's serve."

My betting partner shook his head. "No way. Becker needs to fight as hard as possible now to stay in the set. In this kind of heat, he has to win in straight sets or lose the match."

Being a good sport, Phil gave me the same three-to-one odds that I had been giving him, and sure enough, Chang broke Becker and the set was over. My pile of tennis balls swelled noticeably.

I already knew what my next bet would be. I was certain that the best time for Becker to break Chang in the fourth set would be in the very first game, because the natural tendency for Chang—for any player—would be to relax his guard for a few moments after pulling back a set.

In the mind of a professional tennis player it's quite something to stay alive in the third set after lagging two behind. There's a sense of relief because now you know that, even if you don't win the match, at least you won't make a complete fool of yourself. You won't go home naked. The press won't be running headlines like "Becker Stomps Chang." Naturally, there's a moment of satisfaction, relief, and for your opponent this is maybe the very best moment to come up with a break.

"Now Becker is going to break Chang," I ventured, as the fourth set began.

Phil laughed. "You're crazy! Chang is on a roll now," he said, and again gave me three-to-one.

Immediately, Becker went back to his original game plan, which he had executed successfully in the first two sets. He just clicked right into that space, fresh, alert, mixing it up, not making too many risky shots—and broke Chang's serve. He went on to win the fourth set and his first Grand Slam title in five years.

It was almost as if, while losing the third set, Becker created a trap for Chang. Borrowing a strategy from Sun Yat-sen's classic text, *The Art of War,* he gave his opponent the impression he was weakening, but underneath he was totally prepared, just biding his time.

Although Phil was impressed by my ability to read the game, I have to say that these predictions are only probabilities. It's still a gamble. There are no guarantees. Becker could have tried the same strategies and lost if Chang had played an inspired match. Or Becker's ability to execute his ideas could have been fouled up by a few careless shots.

Nevertheless, I would like to use this example to encourage you to explore and discover your own ways of watching tennis. It can be fun to stand up for your own opinions during a match, even if the commentators and the rest of the audience are saying something entirely different.

There are many ways to watch a match. Each one can give you insights into the game of tennis.

TAKING SIDES

There is the straightforward feeling of sympathy or admiration for a particular player. For example, you like Monica Seles more than you like Steffi Graf. Maybe you don't even know why, that's just the way it is. Naturally, you watch the match through partisan eyes, identifying with Seles, wanting her to win, feeling heartened by her winning strokes, disappointed by her errors.

I would say that the vast majority of spectators watch in this way. In fact, there is an automatic tendency—almost a compulsion—to take sides in any competitive sport. Try this experiment: Switch on your TV, find a sporting event, and watch for a few minutes. Even if you have not previously supported either side, even if you don't know either player or team, you will probably find yourself favoring one over the other within a very short time. It just seems to be part of human nature.

THE TECHNICAL APPROACH

There is the technical way to watch: seeing which player has the stronger serve, the better backhand, the more accurate volley. On television, information about this aspect of a match is usually supplied by former tennis stars who act as support commentators, letting you know which player is stronger or weaker in the various departments of the game. They can tell you how Steffi Graf has been working on her net game, how Andre Agassi has been disciplining himself to be less erratic in his rally game.

GRAF VS. SELES

There is also the *deep background* way to watch: knowing the pressures to which a particular player has been exposed, knowing the off-court tensions behind the match that you are watching.

For example, when Steffi Graf played the 1995 U.S. Open at Flushing Meadow, there was a general consensus of opinion that "she can't do it this time" because her personal problems were looming so large. Her father was behind bars in Germany for tax evasion, her own responsibility in the affair was being questioned, she had a chronic back problem, she was reeling from massive media exposure, and she went into the tournament without her usual level of practice and preparation.

People who were aware of all this could watch Graf's matches with a deeper appreciation of her resourcefulness, her determination, and her guts, especially during her crucial, first-round match against Amanda Coetzer, the South African who had just beaten her in the Canadian Open. Graf lost the first set to Coetzer, just as she had in Canada but made a comeback and won the match 6–4 in the third set.

The final was doubly fascinating from a background perspective because it was Monica Seles's first Grand Slam tournament since being stabbed in the back by the deranged Gunther Parche in Hamburg in April 1993.

Although Seles's physical wound was comparatively minor, the impact on her psyche was severe, causing many observers to wonder whether she would ever play on the pro circuit again. But Seles found a man she could trust in Jerry May, a sports-oriented clinical psychologist working out of Reno, Nevada, and after eighteen months of therapy was able to reenter the international tennis arena.

There was a tremendous amount of emotional and psychological investment for both women, and both accomplished a great deal just to reach the final. After her victory, Graf spontaneously commented that this win meant more to her than even her first Grand Slam triumph—and I agree with her. When you knew the background, it was the toughest test of will she could have faced. The same was true for Seles.

AGASSI VS. BECKER

Another interesting contest from a background perspective in 1995 was the rivalry between Andre Agassi and Boris Becker. For five years, Agassi had dogged Becker. Even when the American was the new kid on the pro circuit, playing erratically, losing frequently to other top players, Agassi always managed to show his true potential against Becker, often beating him by a comfortable margin. At first, Becker took it well, almost with amusement, but gradually Agassi became a thorn in the German's side.

By 1995, there was another angle to the story because Andre Agassi and Pete Sampras had become the world's top-ranking players and both were under contract to Nike—the dominant sponsor in world-class tennis—to promote the firm's sports gear.

The Wimbledon final that year was supposed to be Nike's great moment, when its two champion players would slug it out on center court, fighting for the most prestigious Grand Slam trophy, while in the breaks Nike ads would appear on television screens around the world showing the two heroes in action, inspiring young people everywhere to rush out and buy sneakers.

How did this affect Becker's rivalry with Agassi? It has to do with a major sponsor's ability to dictate the tournament schedule. In professional tournaments, even in the early rounds, the top seeds get most exposure on center court—naturally, because these are the players everyone wants to see. The sponsors want them there in the position of maximum visibility, and Nike was pushing for Sampras and Agassi to be continually in the public eye.

But there is a science to match play of which most professionals are acutely aware. Every court is a bit different. The center court may be faster or slower than court number one or number two, the light may be different, the feel of the environment, the size of the crowd, etc. So if you play all your matches on center court, it gives you a distinct advantage over someone who appears there for the first time in the semifinals.

Becker had been complaining for quite a while that the center-court bias in favor of the top seeds had become unfair. Even though he had enjoyed similar privileges in the past, he loudly proclaimed that it was now too much of an advantage for Agassi.

With all this as background, the semifinal at Wimbledon between Agassi and Becker became a fascinating contest, particularly since Becker—at a time when nobody would have given a penny for his chances—was able to beat the American for the first time in five years. He not only enjoyed beating Agassi, he took great pleasure in destroying the "Nike final."

That was the high point of the Wimbledon tournament for Becker, and when Pete Sampras beat him in the final, he did not seem to mind. In fact, Becker laughed as the match ended, much to the disgust of his coach, Nick Bollettieri, who commented that if a player can laugh at the moment of losing a Wimbledon final, then he needs to be bullied and disciplined into taking a more serious competitive attitude.

Agassi was able to take revenge against Becker in the very next tournament, at the U.S. Open, where he beat the German in a grim and unfriendly battle in the semifinals. Both men played high-level tennis so, from a technical point of view, the game could not be faulted, but the court was basically a war zone. They were out to destroy each other.

When Agassi won, he gave a big victory gesture to his clan of supporters in the crowd but barely touched Becker's hand when they met at the net and did not look at him. Agassi went on to meet Sampras in the final—much to Nike's relief.

The Agassi-Becker saga doesn't end there. One year later, when Agassi crashed out of the 1996 Wimbledon tournament in the first round, he blamed his early departure on Becker. Why? Because Becker's complaints about unfair scheduling had resulted in Agassi playing his first round on Number Two Court, where, according to the American, he was barely able to see the lines. No doubt there are more chapters of this story waiting to be written in future tournaments.

MEDIA AND SPONSORS

Incidentally, it is not just corporate sponsors who influence the way tournament schedules are arranged. Major television networks have a keen interest in screening the most popular players at times when the maximum number of viewers are tuning into the tournament. This blew up into a full-scale controversy at the '96 U.S. Open when several players protested that the seeding hierarchy had been unfairly altered, raising Agassi higher than his current position in the world ranking list. The reason for the switch, according to several angry insiders, was to increase the chances of a Sampras-Agassi match on CBS-TV during prime weekend viewing time.

Becker was recovering from an injury and was not among the protesters, but Yevgeni Kafelnikov, the Russian player who a few weeks earlier had won both the singles and doubles titles at the French Open, was so upset—having been bumped from fifth to seventh position—that he packed his bags and flew home.

Television is, without doubt, a major force in determining the style and presentation of international tennis tournaments, especially in the United States where the principle tactic is to focus on American players and their successes. From the marketing point of view, this seems to make sense, especially when you recall that it was TV exposure of U.S. players like Billie Jean King and Jimmy Connors that first captured the American public's attention and transformed tennis into mass-media entertainment.

For sponsors and TV networks alike, it's always a gamble whether their chosen stars will perform according to expectations, but sometimes they really hit the jackpot. For example, it is fascinating to see how the fantasy of one of Nike's TV commercials became actual reality when Agassi met Sampras in the final of the '95 U.S. Open.

In the commercial, a rally develops between the two players and doesn't stop. It goes on and on, with both men running down every ball and sending it back over the net. Seasons pass, snow falls, the court cracks, and plants start growing through it, but the rally continues.

In the final itself, one of the best rallies ever played in tournament history took place between Sampras and Agassi at set point in the first set. The ball traveled across the net twenty-eight times, and in normal circumstances more than half of the shots—by both Sampras and Agassi—would have been outright winners.

Both players seemed to know beforehand where their opponent would hit next, anticipating and running down unbelievable shots. Sometimes the court would be totally open, with Sampras deep in one corner—almost in the audience—and Agassi had yet to hit the ball, yet Sampras's body would already be moving back toward the point where the ball would next arrive.

NOTICING THE ZONE

This rally was a vivid example of two players being "in the zone," as many professional sportsmen call it—a state in which the body responds intuitively to any given situation before the thinking process of the mind is able to pick up hard facts. It's a mysterious phenomenon, because when a player enters the zone, every aspect of his game suddenly shifts into a higher dimension, becoming one smooth, harmonious flow of energy, producing an optimum performance.

This brings me to the fourth and, for me, the most interesting way to watch tennis: noticing when players move into the zone, understanding who is playing from a state of consciousness, an inner space, that is beyond the level normally attained by mental concentration and physical ability.

Of course, in many matches, neither player will be in the zone—it is not such a common phenomenon—but it is possible to watch ordinary matches in a way that will lead you to an appreciation of a player's inner space or state. Then it will be easier to notice the zone experience when it happens.

If you want to watch in this way, you need to be a little bit more detached than is usual for spectators. You need to be uninvolved in terms of wanting one player or the other to win. You also need to forget about the score for a while and what the commentators are telling you.

Then, just by looking at the face of a player—the expression, the tension lines around the mouth and jaw—you can usually tell whether he or she is feeling relaxed inside, playing from a space of inner harmony, or whether there is some internal conflict going on, some kind of struggle that is making this person tense, creating difficulties in performance.

Also, from the way the body moves on the court, from the reflex responses that are so important in tennis, you can see who is feeling at home, at ease, and who is moving in a more jerky, less coordinated manner. This, essentially, is how I was watching the Becker-Chang match. I was seeing both players as energies, noticing when they were relaxed enough to let their energy flow freely, and when they diminished their energy by becoming tense and anxious.

In this context, two words need clarification: *relaxation* and *energy.* When I use the word *relaxed,* I don't mean that a player is slacking off or playing lazily. I use it to indicate a certain ease and fluidity in a player's style and flow of strokes. The player is sharp, alert, totally involved in the match and playing at full power. But he is not tense, not worried, not overdoing it, not forcing himself to make efforts that turn out to be counterproductive.

By *energy* I mean seeing the player as an organism

through which a vital force is flowing and finding expression. Here, you're not looking at details such as the face, the stroke, or the tactics. You're using your eyes in a less focused way, seeing the fluidity of the player's movement around the court, noticing whether it is smooth or erratic.

Watching tennis in this way, you will notice a significant difference from the way you normally view the game: You are not lost in the action; you remain aware of yourself. You are seeing the match, but you are also—in a certain sense—seeing yourself. This is an essential element in developing a Zen approach to tennis.

FEELING THE GAME FROM WITHIN

If this way of watching seems a little difficult, there are easier ways to approach the same state of mind. Next time you watch a match, whether it is on television, at your local club, or on center court, try something new: Feel the game from within. Feel what it does to you. Take a comfortable position in your chair, watch the game for a few minutes, and then, when you're ready, close your eyes and feel what is happening inside you. What is this match doing to you? How do you feel about the players?

You will get in touch with some unusual insights. For example, when I watched Steffi Graf play in the final of the German Open in Berlin in 1996, I was able to feel—beneath her control and power—her sadness. Even though Graf won, her opponent, Karina Habsudova, was in a happier mood throughout the match and also afterward.

Tuning in, feeling from within, you may realize that you are appreciating the grace of a particular player or the spirit and courage of a fighter who comes back from behind to take a set. To feel these qualities in a player, there also needs to be a place within you that resonates with these qualities. You must have these qualities; otherwise, how could you be aware of them in another person?

If you have the understanding that the players are reflecting something in you, then you can leave a match feeling more in touch with your own courage, your own grace in movement, your own totality. It's a feeling of being uplifted by what you have seen, although naturally this will happen only when the match itself contains some inspirational qualities.

SAMPRAS VS. COURIER

The most memorable, talked-about match of the 1995 season was the quarterfinal of the Australian Open in which Pete Sampras played Jim Courier. At that time Courier was enjoying something of a comeback in his professional career—after a slump of two years—and he was leading Sampras two sets to love.

Then somebody in the crowd shouted to Sampras, "Win one for the Gipper!" and Sampras started crying. The reason, as many people knew, was that Sampras's coach, Tim Gullikson, had been diagnosed with brain cancer and did not have long to live. In other words, Sampras was being encouraged to win the match for his dying coach.

Two remarkable things happened. First, Sampras started shooting aces through his tears. He tried wiping his eyes before each serve, but he was weeping so strongly that more tears immediately replaced them. In professional tennis there is only a twenty-five-second gap permitted between each point, then you have to get on with it, so Sampras was simply throwing up the ball and hitting it almost blindly—and many times hitting an ace.

Courier, on the receiving end, knew he needed only to get the ball back over the net to win the point because Sampras couldn't see, but when the aces kept coming, he just stood there and smiled. He knew it was as remarkable as hitting the right number on a roulette wheel not once but many times.

Courier had been playing like a bull before but became noticeably more friendly when he saw Sampras crying. Maybe, unconsciously, he even helped Sampras to reenter the match, which then became a highly enjoyable and memorable event. Sampras ended up playing at his very best and won the match. He had cried his pain through. Whatever knots had been inside him were dissolved.

In this match, Sampras and Courier were not trying to destroy each other. They both played at a very high level of skill and artistry and with a loving heart. This is a rare phenomenon, but it happens, and when it does, it is an inspiring experience. It transcends the normal level of competition.

Competition gives spice to any sporting event, creating opportunities for athletes to test their skills against each other. But there are layers and layers to any contest and if you remain at a superficial level, becoming preoccupied by the score or by a bias in favor of one of the contestants, you tend to miss the more subtle dimensions. This is a pity, because the deeper you go into a match—as a player or spectator—the deeper you go into yourself, leading ultimately to an experience of Zen.

The Essence of Zen

A scholar was passing a wayside inn where he saw a Zen monk sitting on a stool, eating from a bowl of rice. Thinking this to be a good opportunity to sharpen his skills in argumentation, the scholar approached the monk, sat beside him and, after a short pause, inquired: "What is your essential understanding of Zen?"

"If I could tell you," replied the monk, "it would be my nonessential understanding of Zen."

The scholar was taken aback, but then, after composing himself, asked, "Very well, what is your nonessential understanding of Zen?"

"If it is nonessential," said the monk, "it is not Zen."

The scholar hurriedly departed.

2
Zen:
The Player on the Path

In 1986, Thomas, a friend of mine who is a professional tennis coach, asked me to help one of his students, a fifteen-year-old girl. I accepted his invitation with interest because, although I had been a professional player for several years, I hadn't had much experience coaching other people. To be a good player is one thing; to help someone else raise their game is a totally different kind of challenge.

Thomas said he didn't know how to take the girl further, especially in the domain of match play, where she was having difficulty. So there I was, on court with Ingrid, a shy and insecure teenager who knew she had problems keeping her nerves during a match, and who was now doubly nervous because this stranger had come to "fix" her.

After five minutes of talking with Ingrid, it became obvious that she was already under so much pressure to perform well that whatever words of wisdom I could have shared would not have worked. I knew intuitively that this girl did not need smart, technical advice but some practical experiential support.

Ingrid explained to me that her net game, especially her volleys, would always let her down in crucial moments during a match, so I asked her to hit a few balls with me from the net position while I fed her from the baseline.

As expected, she missed quite a few volleys, even when I presented the ball nicely for an easy shot. What became obvious was how hard Ingrid was trying to do it right, tensing her muscles and making a grimacing expression with her face, as if she was trying to bang nails into concrete.

Immediately she started to complain about herself, saying, "How could I miss such an easy volley?" This soon led to "The truth is, I just can't volley," leading in turn to "I am a hopeless player," leading to—and this she didn't say in so many words— "I am a failure."

Within five minutes of hitting balls we were right there, in the middle of her pain, and she looked at me with frightened eyes because so far, whatever she had done hadn't worked.

EXPERIMENTS IN COACHING

As a player, I had been reading Tim Gallwey's book, a classic in its field, called *The Inner Game of Tennis,* and I decided to experiment with his suggestion to rely on imagery rather than technical instruction as a way of coaching.

"Hit the ball as if you are slapping a mosquito on the wall," I suggested.

"What?" queried Ingrid.

I repeated my suggestion, explaining that you don't put a lot of force and movement into the action of killing a mosquito on a wall. It is more of a quick slap from a close position.

I fed Ingrid more balls. After a while, she got the point, using less effort, relaxing more, and her rate of successful volleys improved slightly.

When I asked her if she was willing to participate in an experiment, she agreed. The exercise was to simply say "hit" whenever her racket connected with the ball. I told Ingrid that this was her only job: simply to say "hit" at the exact moment when the ball touched her racket strings. It was not her job to volley well or to avoid making mistakes.

I fed Ingrid some twenty balls. Sometimes she managed to say "hit" exactly at the moment of impact. More often, she would volley the ball first and say "hit" a split second later. She still missed quite a number of balls.

Then I began asking questions. Each time she volleyed, I'd say something like, "What happened with that last ball? Did you say 'hit' exactly when you hit the ball, or did you say it later?"

In trying to answer these questions, Ingrid became totally absorbed with the exercise, forgetting that she was trying to deal with a volleying problem. Even when she said "hit" exactly at the right time, I kept on questioning her, until suddenly she began to get very excited because she realized that for ten successive balls she had not missed a single volley.

For the first time, her face relaxed into a smile.

"What's happening?" I asked.

"That trick really works!" she replied.

"Let's see."

I gave her another twenty balls, without questioning her, and as I expected, her concentration on the exercise slackened. She started to say "hit" more mechanically, in a routine way, and the number of mistakes increased substantially.

Again, through asking questions, I got her completely absorbed in the exercise and again she managed to hit a high number of balls with less effort and more effectiveness. Through this process Ingrid slowly learned the knack of keeping her attention focused, so that eventually I could stop the questions without affecting her volleying success.

"What are you noticing?" I asked.

She replied, with a kind of humbleness, "Now volleying seems to be easy."

I was as surprised as Ingrid at the dramatic effectiveness of this method, which directs the player's attention toward the physical senses, away from mental activity.

I had not given Ingrid one technical suggestion, one motivational comment such as "Come on, you can do it, try a little harder." I hadn't given one criticism, one word of praise. The only thing I did, in various forms, was to keep on asking the question, "Are you saying 'hit' when you actually hit the ball, or were you early or late?"

A few times I noticed that I wanted to interfere with this simple process by giving the coaching advice that was expected of me, such as "Take the ball earlier," or "Put more weight behind your shot," but I decided not to interfere. I was curious to see how far this revolutionary method could reach.

Within a period of sixty minutes, the improvement of Ingrid's volley in consistency and power was truly amazing, and I felt like I had been part of a miracle.

At the end of the lesson, I asked Ingrid if she could play

with this level of focus in her coming matches, and she replied honestly, "I don't know, but I'll give it a try."

After Ingrid had left, my trainer friend, Thomas, who had been watching the session from some distance so that his presence would not interfere, came up to me and asked, "What did you tell her? She never volleyed so well."

"Nothing," I replied.

"Come on," he said, "you must have taught her many little tricks."

Then I had to admit, honestly, that I only told Ingrid to say "hit" when she hits the ball.

When I heard from Thomas two weeks later that Ingrid had won her first tournament, in the under-eighteen category while she was only fifteen years old, I felt very satisfied. When I saw her a few days after her victory, I congratulated her and asked, "How did you do it?"

She said, "I kept on saying 'hit' when I hit the balls, and not just on the volleys. I did it on all my strokes."

She laughed and added, "In the final, I was so focused on the exercise that I didn't even notice when the match was over. I only understood that I had won from the reactions of the referee, my opponent, and my friends."

NEW INSIGHTS

This experience from my first coaching lesson pushed me onto the path of Zen. It was like a milestone in my search for answers, not only to tennis, but also in a much broader way about the relationship between a person's inner reality and the outer reality that surrounds us.

At the time, I did not consider it to be a spiritual quest,

but I was curious about how our inner attitudes can so dramatically affect outer performance and success. I was especially curious about the functioning of the mind—how it helps us, how it hinders us—and about the wisdom of the human body that at times requires the mind only to be preoccupied in order to come up with the best possible answers.

As far as coaching was concerned, I felt that I had come across a golden key, which, when I was a young player myself, had been missing. In my own training, all of my attention was directed into outer activity, into developing technique: how to perform the correct movements, how to hold the racket, how to bend low before every shot, and so on.

The body was treated like a mechanism that needed to be technically crafted in order to reach a state of optimum performance. And here, in my first coaching session, Ingrid had developed a beautiful volleying movement just from being mentally absorbed while she hit the ball. Once her mind was out of the way, her body performed the movements naturally and perfectly.

A NEW CAREER

My experience with Ingrid launched me into a new career, a three-year period of intense coaching during which I worked with players on all levels, ranging from top professional women—preparing them for Wimbledon, the U.S. Open, and the French Open—to local players who merely wished to improve their performance in their once-a-week social doubles.

In the first six months, I developed dozens of exercises to help players become absorbed by the senses: watching the flight of the ball, feeling the racket, feeling the shift of weight from one foot to another while playing.

My job was mainly to ask questions that helped each player focus on these sensations while the body got on with the job of playing tennis:

"What are you feeling?"

"Where was your racket when the ball landed on your side of the court?"

"How high did your shot pass the net?"

Sometimes, I have to admit, I overdid the questioning technique, becoming so creative in my inquiries that I interfered with the natural rhythm of the person with whom I was playing. I had to learn the delicate art of knowing when it is better to be silent and wait patiently.

TEACHING IN SILENCE

This, in turn, led to another discovery: Some of my students played their best game when I gave them a suggestion and then played with them in silence for a long period, giving them all the space they needed to explore without being disturbed.

This was quite difficult for me to accept. To be silent in a tennis lesson doesn't fit the picture of a good coach. Students usually take a lesson to learn something and for most of us, this means being told what to do and how to do it, then trying to follow these instructions. The trainer's self-value is usually dependent on how much knowledge he possesses and how much he can successfully communicate to the students.

Moreover, the students themselves expect to be taught, and I often found myself in a dilemma, because some people would play beautifully while being left to themselves, but if they lost the magical concentration and began to miss, they would expect technical advice from me, or some play analysis about why they missed a particular shot.

When it was appropriate, I would give such advice, but not in a technical way. For me, it was always a hands-on approach. For example, if somebody was holding his racket awkwardly, I would change the grip, asking, "How does this feel? Better? Would you like to try playing like this for a while?"

More and more, I was able to see the limitations of the conventional teacher-student relationship with its accompanying belief system that there's only one right way to play tennis. The truth is there are many right ways—just like life.

I encouraged my students to understand that when the coach is silent, it doesn't mean he's not doing his job or that he's losing interest. Rather, the opposite is true: He's intentionally creating a space in which the student can explore, experiment, and play freely.

Some of my students very much enjoyed the feeling of a silent yet supportive connection with me as we played, and during these periods they would play their best tennis in a relaxed and effortless way. For both of us, time would cease to exist and the coaching happened in a nonverbal yet extremely powerful way.

I had known such silent, timeless moments as a professional player, during competition matches, when I had moved into the zone. But as a coach, these periods came more frequently and with more power.

I would be playing and suddenly realize that thirty minutes had passed, yet it felt like only five. At these times, I had feelings of being one with the ball, with the court, and with my student. Within my own body, I could almost feel the other person moving—how it must be in his arms, in his legs, as he moves around the court. I could have dismissed all this "weird stuff" but it felt so harmonious and peaceful that I wanted more of it.

HERRIGEL IN JAPAN

It was during this time that I came across *Zen and the Art of Archery*, a beautiful book in which the German philosopher Eugen Herrigel describes his process of becoming a meditator through the discipline of archery.

Herrigel went to Japan in the 1930s to teach philosophy at the University of Kyoto and took the opportunity to visit a Zen master in order to study archery. Herrigel was an accomplished marksman with a pistol before he went to Japan and assumed that he could easily add a little Zen archery to his skills.

The story is that for two years Herrigel tried hard to hit the target, but the Zen master never gave him a sign of acknowledgment. Even worse, at times the master clearly said, "No, you're not getting it."

The master explained to Herrigel that when a Zen archer shoots, he needs to be goalless, empty-minded. He said, "You should not shoot the arrow. The arrow should leave the bow by itself."

With statements like that, Herrigel became more and more frustrated and finally was ready to give up. One day he came to the dojo to give back his bow to the master but had to wait because the master was teaching some other students.

Having accepted that his time with Zen archery was finished, Herrigel was able to watch with an innocent, unprejudiced attitude as the master demonstrated shooting.

He noticed for the first time how relaxed the old man was, how he was not doing it but letting it happen, how he was almost a vehicle, a hollow bamboo, through which the energy of archery could flow and work.

Herrigel was so touched by this insight that he stood up, picked up his bow, and in a state of self-forgetfulness shot a few arrows. The story is that the master whispered in his ear, "That's it. Now you have understood."

TENNIS: A ZEN MEDITATION?

After reading about Herrigel's experiences, I began to wonder if tennis had the potential to be a Zen meditation for me, just as archery had been for him. For example, standing on the court, preparing to serve, I'd ask myself, "How can an ace hit itself, rather than me hitting an ace?"

I didn't have the words then, but this was the beginning of the discovery that I can be a witness to my own actions, a bystander who can watch myself while I am playing. This quality of being a witness, a watcher, has something to do with my state of consciousness. The more conscious I am, the more I can be a witness to myself and to everything that surrounds me. This, in my understanding, is the essence of the Zen approach to meditation.

A lot of people have the idea that meditation is separate from ordinary daily activity, something that you do by sitting down in a quiet room, crossing your legs in the lotus position, closing your eyes, and going inside. In this manner, you watch the thoughts revolving in your mind, you watch any physical sensations in your body, until slowly all thoughts and sensations cease, allowing a deep, inner experience of silence and bliss.

The beauty of the Zen approach to meditation is that it is all-inclusive. It takes ordinary daily activities and turns them into opportunities for meditation, like drinking tea, washing rice, arranging flowers, sweeping the floor . . . or playing tennis. With any activity, you can be as silent and as conscious as if you were sitting alone in a cave in the Himalayas.

However, in trying to apply Zen principles to my game, I soon realized that I needed basic instruction in the art of meditation before attempting to bring it to the tennis court. I couldn't become a Zen player overnight.

I considered a number of options: going to a Zen monastery in Japan, participating in a meditation retreat with the Tibetan Buddhists in Dharmsala, Northern India, or in a Buddhist monastery in Sri Lanka or Thailand. Then a friend who had already been meditating for a number of years suggested a visit to a meditation center in Pune, India, founded by a mystic called Osho.

HEADING EAST

By that time—it was 1991—Osho himself had died, but since I was not looking for a spiritual teacher, this did not deter me. I was more interested in finding practical and effective methods of meditation and experiencing them in a generally supportive atmosphere, talking and sharing with people like myself. I packed my bags and headed East.

In the beginning, the meditation practices taught at the center felt like a lot of work to me. Every morning I participated in a very active meditation that seemed to be more like a fitness workout than something of a spiritual nature.

But in true German fashion, once I had determined to do something, I was not going to give up easily. I performed each meditation as vigorously and as thoroughly as I could. Even when I was participating in the evening meditation, which required nothing more of me than to sit silently, it felt like a test of my willpower not to move a muscle, even when a mosquito would land on my nose.

Soon, in spite of myself, I began to relax. Effortless moments of doing absolutely nothing became more frequent. In these moments, I would simultaneously experience a feeling of deep quietness and self-acceptance.

I could see a connection between the silent spaces I had experienced in my coaching sessions and sitting silently in the meditation hall. Sure, there were obvious differences: On the court I was usually moving around in full activity, and in the meditation hall I was simply sitting. But the inner space, my inner reality, had the same harmonious, timeless quality.

I understood that in my most beautiful and blissful moments on the tennis court I must have been playing in a state of meditation—with no thoughts, no emotions, just crystal-clear awareness. Also, listening to the video and audio recordings of Osho's discourses, I found that my earlier experiences were confirmed by his insights.

Gradually, experiences of meditation started to feel normal to me. In my own way, through tennis, I had knocked on the door of my inner consciousness. Now I had found a method to help me go through the door.

DEVELOPING ZENNIS

The timing of my arrival at the center was fortunate, since a number of sports-oriented people, including a professional tennis coach from Italy, were adding sporting activities to the program. I got involved in developing a meditative tennis workshop, which we playfully decided to call Zennis.

Our basic Zennis workshop lasted three to five days, with each day's schedule consisting of three hours on the tennis court, one hour in a seminar situation where group participants could share their experiences, and three daily meditations.

Specifically, we asked participants to transfer the quiet inner space gained through the meditation techniques into their tennis play on the court. Sometimes, as an added challenge, we would create exercises to disturb them as they played, with people walking around the court, shouting, laughing, cheering, and making comments.

The players who managed this exercise successfully later reported back to us that the effect was spilling over into their daily lives, enabling them to stay relaxed and centered in hectic situations that would otherwise have thrown them off balance.

The sharing meetings were an essential ingredient to the program with many participants reporting new insights triggered by situations on the court. As a direct development of this experience, I have devoted chapter 12 to an explanation of how to create your own Zennis support group so that you can have the opportunity to regularly share your experiences with other players on the path. In my view, sharing your insights with others is one of the most helpful tools in self-understanding.

HEADING WEST

I learned a great deal through developing the Zennis program, but I was also aware that the real test lay outside the meditation center, in what Zen people refer to as "the marketplace" of the ordinary world. Would I be able to convey the discoveries I had made to people who had no particular interest in meditation? It was time to find out. Again, I packed my bags, this time heading West.

Since my return from India, I have been leading Zennis workshops in the United States, Europe, and Australia, and my experience is that the Zen approach to tennis can work with anyone, on any level of the game, with two conditions:

First, that people are willing to look at themselves, at their thoughts, their feelings, and their attitudes so that tennis can be used as a mirror to reflect their inner reality.

Second, that they are willing to share this inner process with me, or with a supportive group of people.

With this willingness, I have found that Zennis helps not only to dramatically improve a person's game but also greatly enhances personal enjoyment of playing. Simultaneously, and almost as a by-product, people begin to look at life in a new way, to see new possibilities of creativity and fulfillment.

GROUND RULES OF MEDITATION

During this time, I have also come to understand some important ground rules of meditation that I would like to share with you before proceeding further. This seems necessary because, since we are intruding into the spiritual realm, we also need to confront common attitudes and beliefs that people share about spirituality and religion.

First, no one has a copyright on meditation. It belongs to everyone. Different teachers have developed different meditation techniques, but all techniques—if they are authentic—lead to the same inner experience of silence, timelessness, peace, and bliss.

Second, this inner experience is available to every human being, regardless of caste, creed, or color. No religious belief system can claim exclusive rights to it and those who are intelligent—like the Zen mystics—don't even try to do so. They simply point the way and encourage adventurous individuals to claim the experience for themselves. These mystics are like fingers pointing to the moon. The point is to reach the moon, not to get attached to a particular finger and start to worship it.

Third, self-discovery is an individual affair. It can be helpful to explore with like-minded people and to meditate in a supportive environment, but each person's path is going to be unique. Your path is discovered only when you walk it. It cannot be determined by others.

These are my basic understandings, gathered from my personal experiences over the past ten years. Bearing these principles in mind, I invite you to explore the fascinating world of Zen and Zen tennis, becoming a player on the path.

How Do You Do It?

*A frog was sitting on a patch of grass by his pond
one sunny morning when a large centipede passed by.
The frog watched this creature with fascination, then
said, "Excuse me, can I ask you a question?"*

*"Why, yes, of course," replied the centipede,
pausing in his stride.*

*"I am amazed at the way you can proceed so
harmoniously with your one hundred legs," said the
frog. "Can you explain to me how you manage to
keep them in order?"*

*The centipede reflected for a moment. "You know,
I have never really thought about it," he said. "Let
me see if I can demonstrate it for you." And he
started to walk, thinking about which leg should follow another. Immediately, he fell down and had great
difficulty getting up again.*

*"You are dangerous!" he said to the frog angrily.
"Never again ask such questions!"*

3
The Zennis Form

One of the benefits that television has brought to spectator sports is the slow-motion replay. Through it, you are able to see crucial moments in a game that would otherwise pass too swiftly to observe properly. You are also able to see, in an almost poetic way, the power, grace, and beauty of the human body in action.

The Zennis form, introduced in this chapter, gives you an opportunity to experience your own slow-motion replay. It is a series of tennis movements performed in a very slow, deliberate way, as if you are moving your body through a medium that is thicker than air, like water or honey.

Slowing down any movement allows you to bring more awareness to it. You can be more conscious of what you are doing. In slow motion, you come to know all the subtle things that are happening inside your body during even a simple movement like sitting down in a chair or walking along the street.

ROOTS OF THE FORM

Before you begin to learn the Zennis form, however, it will be useful to know something about its origins. It is derived from the ancient Chinese art of tai chi, which was developed as a form of self-defense and later became an effective method of centering and meditation.

Tai chi is a series of movements designed so that a single individual can deal with multiple attacks coming from different directions while maintaining a sense of balance and composure. It is performed in slow motion, almost like a dance or ballet. Special emphasis is given to the hara, the body's central balance point, located three finger widths below the navel.

Tai chi helps to quiet your mind, maintain your physical health, and give you a strong sense of the way energy flows through your body. This vital energy is known as *chi*.

FLOW OF CHI ENERGY

When I first started learning tai chi, I practiced a series of basic warm-up exercises designed to generate chi and help it move through the body. What I experienced, especially in the beginning, was that in certain parts of my body, the energy was blocked. For example, in my right leg it would not reach below my knee. One exercise was particularly helpful in burning through these blocks, and I will describe it in detail on page 43 so that you can try it for yourself.

After a few days of doing this simple exercise, I could feel the chi flowing evenly throughout my body and had a strong sensation of this vital energy shooting out of my hands. In fact, one of my chief memories from that introductory experience was the sensation of how warm my hands were throughout the practice sessions.

Since my hands are accustomed to holding rackets, I realized that this chi energy, once incorporated into tennis, could make my game more powerful and economical. It also occurred to me that a player whose energy flows smoothly and powerfully to the hands is unlikely to suffer from the common problem of tennis elbow.

Tennis elbow is caused by the incorrect use of muscle power. On a micro level, strong, jerky arm movements cause tiny tears in the tissue fiber of the tendons. When these heal, the tendon is slightly shortened and is no longer as elastic, resulting in pain each time a player tries to make a stroke.

A player who learns to feel the flow of chi throughout his body has a better chance of avoiding tendon and muscle damage; first, because the even flow of energy will maintain a higher standard of health and tone; second, because he will be using the increased energy to do work that otherwise would be left entirely to the muscles.

BEING GROUNDED

Through tai chi, I learned how important it is to be grounded, to feel a strong connection to the earth. This is experienced through maintaining a low center of gravity—knees unlocked, belly relaxed, and the soles of your feet flat on the ground.

Our normal, habitual way of standing is with straight

legs, chest out, belly held in, with the buttocks pressed to-gether, rather like a soldier on parade. This is our idea of appearing to be strong, as a soldier needs to appear in order to intimidate the enemy. In this position the breathing is confined mainly to the upper chest.

In tai chi, the position of maximum power and strength is almost the polar opposite of the soldier's stance, and it is worth exploring because when you begin to experience other possibilities, it can radically change your assumptions about strength and weakness.

If you unlock your knees and sink down, by bending your legs slightly, then your buttocks start to relax, your belly comes out, and your shoulders and arms can hang loosely by your sides.

Your breathing can travel down through your chest into your belly. By the way, when I say this, I don't mean that it happens physiologically. Breathing, of course, takes place in your lungs, not in your belly. But the *feeling* of breathing into your belly is very different from breathing into your chest and the effects are also different.

From this relaxed position, you can respond with real agility and flexibility. Try it, and you will find that you are more centered and cannot be easily pushed over or knocked off balance. You can turn smoothly and quickly from one side to the other. You can move forward into the attack, or you can prepare to receive an attack from an opponent.

RECEIVING AND RETURNING ENERGY

In tai chi you don't merely resist an attack. The idea is to receive the energy of the incoming attacker and transform it in a way so that you can send the energy back. You use the energy directed at you to make a stronger counterattack. It is an illustration of the Eastern wisdom of yin and yang, in which opposing energies—for example, attack and defense, aggression and receptivity—can become complementary to each other.

Transferring this principle to the game of tennis, I understood that people who have problems in responding to powerful shots, such as an opponent's strong first serve, do not understand that they can receive the energy of the approaching ball, absorb this energy into the body, and then send it back. Instead, they respond by becoming very tense, with rigid muscles, a tight belly and chest, relying only on the power of their arm muscles to reply. This usually leads to a weak and unsatisfactory return shot, and it heightens the chances of injuries like tennis elbow.

When I experimented with tai chi as a way of dealing with aggressive energy, I would say to myself, "The harder the serve approaches me, the more loose and liquid I remain." Instead of feeling that I was defending myself against the ball, I imagined that I was receiving it, welcoming the energy that was coming toward me, thankful that I did not have to generate all that power but only return it to my opponent.

On a scientific level, what I have just described—receiving and absorbing energy, then sending it back—may seem implausible. When top professionals play, only 0.5 seconds elapse between the moment the ball leaves the server's racket and the moment it hits the returner's racket. On impact, the ball stays on the racket strings for about one-hundredth of a second. So, when I am facing a serve, there is no time for me to think, "Now I am welcoming the ball." As the ball hits my racket there is no time to think, "Now I am receiving and returning the energy."

All this happens spontaneously, intuitively. It cannot be done with mental deliberation. It is more like an inner image, an inner attitude. The body, following the image of receptivity, has its own ways to feel that it is absorbing energy, especially when it is relaxed. It does not need to hear the mind recite the words in order to perform the function.

TAI CHI AND TENNIS: SIMILARITIES

The main portion of any tai chi course is learning what is known as *the form,* a sequence of movements performed in all directions, sometimes as you are moving forward, sometimes backward, continuously changing your body position. These movements all serve the basic purpose of being able to deal with imagined attacks occurring from all directions and from all levels.

While I was practicing the tai chi form, I noticed that many of the movements are similar to those we use in tennis. On the court, you move forward to the net and back to the baseline. You have movements on the right side of your body—if you are right-handed, that's your forehand; and on the left side, it's your backhand. You have to make high, overhead smashes and deal with low, bouncing shots. And at any given moment you need to be prepared for all of these moves.

One thing is missing: fortunately, a tennis player does not need to anticipate attacks coming from behind, but that's about the only exception (unless you happen to play Davis Cup against Italy in Rome, where some spectators throw coins at you from behind).

The Zennis form, derived from tai chi, is a series of movements that incorporates all the basic tennis strokes: beginning with a neutral stance, then moving into a forehand followed by a backhand, then a forehand volley followed by a backhand volley, and finishing with an overhead smash.

Like tai chi, the Zennis form gives emphasis to many details, like the shift of weight from one foot to another, the focus of your awareness on your balance point, what happens in your pelvis as you move, how to generate more energy, and so on. It is done very slowly, as if you are participating in a slow-motion replay on television or playing underwater aqua-tennis.

TEACHING THE ZENNIS FORM

In the tradition of Zen, it's almost a *faux pas* to teach in a purely descriptive way. If you are with a Zen master learning archery or some kind of martial art, he may sometimes give verbal instructions but on other occasions he may merely touch your arm and, without explaining anything, put you in the right position, bypassing your rational mind. Through this kind of nonverbal transmission a deeper understanding happens and remembrance of the position comes automatically each time you perform the movement.

Sometimes the master may not do anything, because he sees the time is ripe for the student to repeat a certain movement hundreds of times until it becomes second nature. On another occasion, seeing that a student is trying too hard, making too much mental effort, he may ask him to focus his attention on his breathing, thereby keeping the mind occupied while the body naturally performs the sequence of movements.

In a book, such subtle forms of teaching are not available. There is no alternative but to rely on a description of the Zennis form. However, I have tried to keep it as simple as possible, and I encourage you to rely on your natural feeling for each of the strokes, using your own style of play, incorporating these instructions without turning them into rigid rules.

Questions may arise about the precise position of your body and your racket. This is understandable but actually not so important in this context. The main emphasis is on slowing down your strokes and becoming more aware of your body and its movements. In this way, you will begin to develop your own rhythm and flow. Remember, in Zen, the path itself is the goal. You are not being asked to develop the perfect Zennis form but to become more aware of what is happening to you now, in the present moment.

Some practical suggestions: You can do the Zennis form anywhere. Some people may enjoy doing the form on a tennis court, others in their room. You can do it alone or with friends. If you do it with another person, your partner can read the instructions aloud while you follow them; then you can switch roles. I will describe the movements as if you are holding a tennis racket, but you can also simply imagine that you are holding one. The effect will be the same.

WARM-UP EXERCISE

This exercise, which I mentioned earlier, promotes the flow of chi through your body and also helps to open any blocks that may be inhibiting energy flow.

Wear loose, comfortable clothing.

Your belly should be relaxed and not restricted by a tight belt or strong elastic.

Stand loosely and relaxed, with your feet shoulder width

apart, bend your knees, and sink down into your legs while keeping your spine straight. In this low position, you allow your pelvis to drop down and forward so that your lower back is not arched.

Maintain this position for a few minutes—start with two minutes and work up to five—breathing slowly and deeply. Make sure that your breathing does not only make your chest rise and fall but also your belly.

Within a short time, certain areas of your body will begin to shake or tremble, especially your legs. You may also experience a few aches and pains. This is a sign that you are generating chi, but the flow of energy is being blocked by muscle tension.

When this exercise is practiced regularly for a few minutes each day, you can feel the chi starting to open the energy blocks. Soon, the muscles will open and relax, allowing the chi to pass naturally through them, and you will feel the difference in your whole body: sensations of warmth, vitality, and circulating energy. It is a very healthy feeling.

Practice this exercise for ten days continuously.

The Neutral Stance

In tai chi, the place to focus while you are receiving and sending energy is the hara center, which, as I mentioned earlier, is located in your lower belly. In Japan, the hara has been known for centuries as the body's central point of balance, a source of vital energy, and also a center of instinctive intelligence.

In Western countries, we do not have the same understanding about the hara, but we pay tribute to it when we say things like "He's playing from his guts," when describing a player's gritty performance, or "I have a gut feeling about . . ." when we have a certain feeling that we are sure is true but that we cannot prove through rational, intellectual analysis.

In the Zennis form, it is important to adopt the neutral stance after each stroke so that you can remain centered in your hara, able to respond continuously and flexibly to what is happening on the court while maintaining your balance. In a holistic sense, this position also promotes the feeling that your body, mind, and emotions are integrated and working harmoniously together.

If you are doing this exercise on a tennis court, stand at the midpoint of the baseline. If you do it in your room, you will need a little space to the left and right and in front of you to accommodate the strokes that follow.

Here, then, is the neutral stance:

Stand with your feet parallel, shoulder width apart. It is the outside edges of your feet that are parallel, so you may appear to be slightly pigeon-toed. Relax in your knees and let your legs bend slightly, so that you sink down a couple of inches in overall height.

As you do so, you will notice that your belly automatically relaxes. Make sure that your buttocks are also relaxed, your lower back is not arched, and your pelvis is dropped down and forward.

Look straight ahead, as if facing an opponent across the net.

Allow your shoulders to relax and also your jaw, mouth, and tongue. (It may sound strange, but many champions allow their tongues to hang out when they play their best tennis, including Sampras, Becker, and McEnroe. Agassi and the media called Sampras a "monkey" for doing it before

Sampras became the ruling emperor of the pro tour, but it simply shows how relaxed he can be, since it takes muscular effort to keep the mouth closed.)

Hold your racket in front of you, aligned with the middle of your body, pointing out at a forty-five-degree angle from your body, with the racket head higher than the grip. Your shoulders are relaxed. Your elbows are slightly bent, close to your body.

Your right hand holds the racket grip with just enough effort to control the racket. Your left hand holds the neck of the racket, just below the head. Many people don't play their best tennis because they grip the racket too hard. You should hold it rather like holding a little bird: Don't let the bird fly away, but don't squeeze it.

Pay attention to your breathing. Let it be slow and deep. Focus your awareness in your hara. Feel your feet flat on the ground. Perhaps you can visualize an image of growing roots down through your feet into the earth. This will help you gain a feeling of being solidly grounded.

This is the neutral stance. Explore the position by letting your upper body and pelvis move slightly, turning to the left and right. Notice how these movements have the lower belly as their focal point.

Stay in the neutral stance for a few minutes until you feel comfortable with this position.

The Forehand

As you move through the forehand stroke, I want you to focus your attention on moving slowly, noticing how your weight shifts from foot to foot. Don't worry about the details and getting the stroke exactly right. Have the idea that you are going to do your usual forehand.

Begin with the neutral stance.

Stand in a relaxed way, imagining that you are on the court, looking toward the net, facing an opponent.

Your feet are parallel, and your weight is distributed evenly on both feet. You have the feeling of being slightly pigeon-toed. Your knees are slightly bent.

Shift your weight to your left foot, and with your right foot step out at a forty-five-degree angle to the right side of you body.

Slowly shift your weight to your right foot, with the trunk of your body rotating naturally to the right.

Your racket is next to your body and moves to the right simply because you have rotated your trunk. Your left hand is connected with the neck of your racket.

Now your weight shifts more to your right foot and your racket moves back and low, with your left hand separating from the racket and your eyes looking out ahead, as if watching the oncoming ball.

Step forward with your left foot in a straight line from its original position, not across the body. Let the heel of your foot touch the ground first, as if testing ice on a river to see if it can take your weight.

Your weight distribution is now approximately 80 percent on your back foot (right foot) and 20 percent on your front foot (left foot).

Your weight shifts slowly from your back foot to your front foot while at the same time your hips are rotating forward to face the net. Simultaneously, your racket swings slowly forward and upward from its lowest point behind you to a meeting point with the ball in front and to the side of your body.

Your racket flows through the point of contact with the ball and moves up over your left shoulder, pointing behind you.

Now your right foot moves forward parallel to your left foot, and you find yourself again in the neutral stance, ready to meet the next shot from your opponent.

The Backhand

As with the forehand, do not be overly concerned with the technical precision of the backhand stroke that you are about to make. Focus your attention on moving slowly and noticing the shift of weight from foot to foot.

Begin in the neutral stance. Your knees are slightly bent; your feet are parallel.

Relax by taking a deep breath and exhaling slowly.

Shift your weight to your right foot, and step out with your left foot at a forty-five-degree angle from your body.

Slowly, your weight shifts onto your left foot and your upper body rotates naturally to the left. Your racket is next to your body, and you are lightly holding the neck with your left hand.

You continue to look out ahead toward the net.

All the weight shifts to your left foot, and you step out in a straight line toward the net with your right foot. Your heel touches the ground first.

In this position, 80 percent of your weight is on your left foot, and 20 percent is in your right heel.

Shift your weight from your back foot (left foot) to your front foot (right foot). Simultaneously, your racket drops to its lowest point and swings slowly forward and upward, through the meeting point with the ball.

Your left arm stays behind your body, and there is a feeling of opening and expanding your chest. There should be a sense of freedom and release as you follow through with this stroke.

Your backhand stroke ends with your racket held high to the side of your right shoulder.

Your left foot steps forward, parallel to your right foot, bringing you again into the neutral stance.

The Forehand Volley

The forehand volley is a short and compact movement.

Begin in the neutral stance, sinking a little lower than before. Both elbows are in front of your body, closer together than in the forehand and backhand movements.

Shift your weight slowly to your left foot, and with your right foot take a small step at a forty-five-degree angle from your body.

Your upper body rotates to the right, taking your arms and racket with it.

Shift your weight onto your right foot.

As your right foot takes your weight, with your racket in front of you, your left foot steps out in a straight line forward onto the heel.

Push with your back foot (right foot) so that your weight starts shifting onto your front foot (left foot), and as you do so, let your hips come parallel with the net.

Your racket follows the movement of your hips through the point of impact with the ball but not far beyond it.

While following through, your racket moves in a straight line toward the net.

At the end of your stroke, all your weight is on your left foot.

Take a step forward with your right foot so that your feet are parallel.

As you do so, allow your arms to return to their position in the neutral stance.

In a sense, the volley is played more with your legs than with your arms. There is no big swing. The power comes through your legs and the shift of weight.

The Backhand Volley

Begin in the neutral stance, sinking low as with the forehand volley. Elbows are in front of your body, closer together than with the forehand and backhand movements.

Slowly shift your weight to your right foot.

With your left foot, take a small step at a forty-five-degree angle from your body.

As you do so, let your trunk turn from your hips toward the left side, taking your arms and racket with it.

Shift your weight from your right foot to your left foot.

All the weight is now on your left foot.

Your face is toward the net.

Step forward with your right foot in a straight line, heel first.

Push from your back foot (left foot) into your front foot (right foot), shifting your weight.

Your racket pushes through the point of impact with the ball, but not very far. During this action, your shoulders remain sideways to the net. Your left hand stays back to stabilize the forward thrust.

Your racket follows through in the direction of the ball. It does not curve around your body.

At the end of the stroke, all your weight is on your right foot.

Take a step forward with your left foot so that your feet are parallel.

This movement naturally rotates your upper body to face forward, coming into the neutral stance.

Overhead Smash

Begin with the neutral stance, sinking low, as if you are expecting to volley.

Both elbows are in front of your body, closer together than with the forehand and backhand movements.

Shift your weight slowly to your left foot.

Step back with your right foot, your toes pointing out at a forty-five-degree angle.

As you do so, your hips and shoulders turn to the right.

With the rotation of your upper body, your left arm rises up, your hand pointing to the high ball that is approaching.

You raise your right elbow to shoulder level, so that your racket is lifted behind your head, with the racket head pointing straight up.

About 80 percent of your weight is now on your back foot (right foot).

From here, the forward motion starts: Shift your weight from your right foot onto your left foot. At the same time, let your racket head drop low behind you, as if scratching your back.

As you push forward with your back foot, your back heel leaves the ground and your hips turn parallel with the net.

Bring your racket forward and upward to a point of full extension above your head, slightly on your right side.

Your left elbow tucks into your body. This will prevent your body from rotating too far around to the left.

As your racket comes forward, let the strings of your racket meet the ball square on at the moment of impact. The follow-through is short.

All your weight is on your left foot at the end of the stroke.

Step forward with your right foot to a parallel position with your left foot, returning to the neutral stance.

BREATHING

The breathing is the same for all movements.

Each movement is completed with a single breath: one inhale and one exhale.

In the neutral stance, inhale deeply into your belly.

With the beginning of the stroke, gently begin to exhale.

Time your exhale so that, when you come to the moment of contact with the ball, you have exhaled about 60 percent of the air in your lungs.

At the moment of impact, fully exhale the remaining 40 percent of air.

Return to the neutral stance.

Inhale deeply and then begin the next movement.

Bringing your attention to your breathing will help you to develop smooth movements. It will also allow you to do the Zennis form in a relaxed, healthy, and meditative way.

When you are in the process of learning the form, even

when forgetting some of the instructions, you will immediately feel the benefits of this technique if you breathe in a harmonious way.

You will end feeling refreshed and vital.

DIFFERENT AREAS OF FOCUS

In the same way that tai chi began as a form of self-defense and became valued as a method of meditation, the Zennis form can become one of your meditation techniques—something you give to yourself as a way of staying centered, relaxed, and alert within the context of your daily life.

Practicing the Zennis form over a period of weeks, you can focus your attention on different details. For example, you can begin by bringing more awareness to the position and movement of your feet: how they are anchored, how they create a feeling of being grounded, giving you strong roots in the earth.

Next, you can focus your attention on your hara center, feeling the body's balance point as you move through the form.

Then you can switch focus to your chest and shoulders, because they naturally follow the movement of your belly—they are always slightly behind.

Finally, you can focus on the path the racket takes.

In this way, you will experience in detail the chain reaction of movement, beginning with the feet and ending in your racket.

It is also helpful to practice occasionally in front of a mirror so that you can see yourself as you move.

Remember, you can also do the form without your tennis racket. Open your hands while doing the movements and imagine you are hitting the ball with your hand.

DAILY PRACTICE

Once you feel comfortable with each movement, you can practice the Zennis form as a continuous, integrated series, repeating it many times in an even, flowing rhythm.

Beginning with the neutral stance, the sequence should take about 70 to 100 seconds to complete. As you return for the last time to the neutral stance, stand quietly, inhale deeply, and then exhale in a slow, relaxed manner.

Take a short break of about twenty to thirty seconds between each sequence, allowing yourself to feel loose and relaxed—maybe shaking your feet and legs slightly—before adopting the neutral stance and beginning the Zennis form again.

As a daily practice, it is good to perform the sequence five times, which takes about ten minutes. This can be very helpful before playing a match and can also help you stay in tune with your game on days when you do not play.

INCORPORATING THE FORM INTO YOUR GAME

The Zennis form is done in slow motion. However, when you play a match, you are moving at full speed. How do you incorporate these slow movements into the fast pace of a tennis match?

My suggestion is simple: Do not try to incorporate them. By repeating the Zennis form on a daily basis, the movements will be absorbed and understood by your body, which will adopt them on court without thinking. This will naturally lead to a more fluid and powerful style of play.

In addition, your body becomes so finely tuned that even when you make a mistake, it will give you immediate feedback on what went wrong. You start feeling when your weight shifts too early or when you lean in too much. You will start learning important lessons that would otherwise be available only from a good coach.

You will also start to feel the chi energy flowing out of your hands and experience the resulting increase in power. You do not have to consciously direct the energy into your hands in order to have this experience. It happens by itself.

The Lottery Money

A professor of religion once visited a well-known mystic and spent several days listening to his discourses. He found many inconsistencies and inaccuracies in the mystic's talks, and, when the two men met, he pointed out the errors, one by one.

The mystic waited politely until the professor had finished, then remarked, "Your attitude reminds me of a story." He then proceeded to tell the following tale:

A poor shoemaker entered a lottery and won a great deal of money.

"How did you manage it?" asked an envious customer the next day.

"It was quite simple," replied the shoemaker. "I am fond of the number nine, so I selected those numbers that are multiples of nine: eighteen, twenty-seven, thirty-six, forty-four . . ."

"Wait a minute, you have made a mistake," interrupted the customer, "the number forty-four is not a multiple of nine."

The shoemaker thought for a moment. "Ah, well," he replied. "You have the arithmetic, I have the lottery money."

4

Seven Unusual Exercises for Zennis

There are a number of practical and effective exercises for the Zennis player that I would like to share with you. These exercises will help you to play better tennis and also support you in moving toward the inner state that Zen people call *No Mind*, or *Mind* with a capital *M*, a space of silence and stillness where the normal, continuous thinking process of the mind has temporarily ceased.

As I mentioned earlier, many tennis professionals experience glimpses of this state and refer to it as playing in the zone. Getting into this state tends to happen during intense moments of play when there is a heightened sense of harmony within yourself and also with your surroundings.

Players say that, in the zone, they know beforehand where the balls are going to land. They also report that tennis balls often seem bigger than normal size and travel at much slower speeds, as if they are playing with huge tennis balls in slow motion.

Through doing these exercises, you may not necessarily encounter the same phenomena, but you will definitely experience the game of tennis from unusual perspectives. Let me encourage you to temporarily put aside your ideas of how tennis should be played and explore these seven exercises in an open-minded and curious way.

All exercises require a playing partner on the court. Some need a third person as well. The final exercise is for a doubles match.

The "Stop!" Exercise

Participants: two players, one helper.
Purpose: developing your ability to be detached from winning and losing.

Make an agreement with your playing partner that you both want to incorporate this exercise into a tennis match.

The exercise begins with you and your partner warming up on the court, then starting to play a match.

The third person, the helper—let's call him Ted—is watching from an umpire position.

Ted's job is to shout "Stop!" unexpectedly at any moment during your match.

Immediately, you and your playing partner will stop playing and stand on the court as if frozen into statues, with eyes closed.

Ted waits for about thirty seconds and then says, "Okay, you can continue playing."

Resume the match, replaying the point that was in progress when Ted gave the instruction.

The command "Stop!" is given three to five times within thirty minutes.

The exercise is very simple, but also very powerful.

For example, imagine you are in the middle of an intense rally, chasing a wide ball to your forehand, maybe already figuring out an appropriate response, such as playing a high ball to your partner's backhand. You are deep in the game, running toward the ball, and suddenly Ted shouts, "Stop!"

It's fine for you to take one or two steps to come to a halt, but do not finish your stroke. Stop as quickly as possible and stand frozen in whatever position you find yourself.

Close your eyes and be aware of any sensations you may be feeling in your body and also any thoughts passing through your mind. In this moment, you may simply experience silence, or you may be aware of other things: the blood pumping in your veins, the sweat on your body, the tension in your legs.

You may see your mind as separate from yourself, like a chattering monkey inside your head. You may hear your competitive mind saying, "Dammit! Why did Ted have to say 'Stop!' now, just when I was going for a winner," or maybe, "Nice timing, Ted! I was going to lose that point."

Sometimes players are so hooked into the match that they want to continue playing and complete the stroke, even when the command "Stop!" was given well beforehand.

On one occasion, in a doubles match, I shouted "Stop!" loudly, then watched as three players froze immediately and one continued to run across the court until he could hit the ball and send it back over the net. Only then did he stop. Later, he became embarrassed by his action and swore that he hadn't heard the shout.

For such people, it's instructional for them to note, as

they stand on the court with closed eyes, what is driving them to deny the exercise. Maybe it's a certain stubbornness—"I'm going to play this match my way"—or maybe the competitive urge is too strong and winning has become the most important thing.

Ted can also shout "Stop!" during moments of the match that are normally dismissed as of no consequence, such as during the changeover or when players are picking up balls in corners of the court.

This can also be a valuable experience. For example, one participant in this exercise, Jennifer, told me that previously she had always perceived such moments as a break from "the real thing," during which she tended to "switch off" and do things mechanically. When asked how this habit translated into her daily life, Jennifer acknowledged that she had the same basic attitude: much of her day was dismissed as humdrum and only in special moments did she allow herself to come fully alive and alert.

Through the exercise, Jennifer felt encouraged to bring more vitality and consciousness to the ordinary moments that make up the bulk of her daily life.

Generally, players are quick to notice a different quality within themselves after experiencing the "Stop!" exercise. They play more consciously and spontaneously, less from habit, and—especially in doubles matches—the atmosphere becomes noticeably more friendly and harmonious.

Personally, I find this exercise to be one of the most powerful tools for helping people gain insights into their nature. The "Stop!" is such a sudden break with reality that it becomes a modern equivalent of the traditional Zen stick, when disciples would be unexpectedly hit by the master's staff—a device through which many seekers became enlightened.

After the match, it can be helpful for the players to reflect on what they have experienced through this exercise and then share these experiences with each other.

Disturbing the Match

Participants: two players, one helper, and possibly a group of friends.

Purpose: staying centered and focused amid external distractions.

Materials needed: extra tennis balls for the helper.

We have all seen matches, either on television or live, during which players were disturbed by off-court situations, such as spectators standing up in the middle of a rally or making comments about the play or starting to clap or boo while play is continuing.

At club level, it can also happen that a player from a nearby court will come too close to you in order to pick up a stray ball, interfering with your game.

In this exercise I invite you to be deliberately disturbed during a match, and to discover how a so-called disturbance can make you more focused on your game. The trick is to go inside and become a witness to the disturbance. This doesn't happen overnight, but with a little practice you can transform an apparent problem into an opportunity.

Again, you need the help of a third party, and again, we will call on Ted for assistance.

Begin to play a match with your partner, agreeing beforehand to incorporate this exercise.

Ted's job is to roll or toss balls onto the court in front of the players. He can do this at any time, either when you are about to serve or while a rally is in progress.

Ted can also talk to you, making positive or negative comments about how you are playing—the slice on your backhand for example—or perhaps about some business appointment that awaits you after the match. Any kind of comment will do.

He can also start to clap or shout his support for you or your opponent.

Your challenge is to find a place inside that is independent of these outside activities. This is a knack that you acquire rather than a skill that can be taught, but a few things will be helpful:

First, remember that you are playing this match to experience the exercise, not to win or lose nor to prove anything about your playing abilities.

Second, play as well as you can, but remain playful, keep a sense of humor.

Third, whenever you remember, keep the focus of your attention inside yourself rather than on the play. This can be done by paying attention to your breathing or by feeling the grip of your hand on the racket or by remaining aware of the balance point in your belly.

These techniques help to switch your attention from your mind to your kinesthetic senses, and slowly you will develop the ability to remain undisturbed by what is happening around you.

For Ted, there is one safety factor to remember while disturbing the game: always roll or toss balls well in front of the players, so that they see them clearly; otherwise, someone may accidentally step on a ball and fall. It is best to roll balls while the players are at the baseline. Never roll a ball behind a player. Throw your balls so that they bounce clear across the court and do not remain within the playing area.

There are several variations on the theme of this exercise.

If you have the chance to get a group of friends together, you can try playing in front of a crowd that is at first positive and then negative toward one player or the other. This can involve cheering, booing, and open encouragement or criticism.

One of the greatest challenges for a male player is to invite female friends to mother him from the sidelines while he plays. This can be a beautiful and playful test, especially in front of other men. Women players can also be mothered.

In my personal experience, famous lines from girlfriends in such situations include:

"Did you put your sunblock on? You know your skin is too delicate for direct sunlight."

"Why don't wear your hat? I told you to wear your hat."

"Don't run so much, darling, you will be tired later."

If you want the ultimate challenge, you can invite your real mother to come and do the same. If you manage to stay centered and focused in such a situation, then you are a true master of Zen tennis.

For an additional exercise for women players, you may want to invite a couple of male friends to watch and make comments like "She looks kinda cute when she's out of breath, doesn't she?"

Be creative, be playful, be loving. There is no need to say anything that is wounding or hurtful.

Hitting Out

Participants: two players.

Purpose: going beyond the fear of making mistakes and gaining confidence in your natural swing.

In this exercise I invite you to deliberately hit the ball beyond the baseline.

Usually, the baseline is associated with fear. This is understandable because if you hit beyond the line during a match, you lose the point.

On the other hand, a basic requirement for a good player is to be able to hit the ball close to the baseline, since this keeps your opponent under pressure and allows you to stay in control of the game.

To hit the ball out will help you to swing freely and go beyond your fear of making mistakes.

Practice with a partner, who we will call Nick.

Ask Nick to feed you balls from the other end of the court. As he does so, make sure that you hit each and every ball beyond the baseline.

If, once in a while, you don't make it and the ball lands inside the court, Nick needs to encourage you to keep hitting out.

After five minutes of encouragement, Nick continues to feed balls to you, but now he can become quiet. Let the experiment unfold naturally. If your balls start to be a bit shorter now, or if they continue to go out, it does not matter.

After ten minutes, change roles.

Now you feed balls to Nick and it is his turn to hit out.

I notice with this exercise that, after a few sessions, students start hitting the ball inside the court at perfect length, maybe a foot from the baseline. By losing the fear of hitting out, their bodies relax, and a natural rhythm of swinging the racket for a baseline shot takes over, producing balls of optimum length.

The same effect is possible when you practice serving.

You can deliberately hit beyond the serve line until your natural rhythm takes over.

One by-product of this exercise is that you will stop hitting into the net, and this will give you an advantage in any match. It is worth noting that about 70 percent of errors on the tennis court result from the ball landing in the net, not outside the field of play. So, if you master the art of playing most of your balls over the net, you are already a successful player.

In my view, it's also healthier to hit the ball long than to hit it into the net. Hitting out allows you to develop a free and natural swing. Hitting into the net usually happens because you are swinging in a tense and overly controlled manner.

In addition, this exercise helps you to develop a style of swinging at the ball, not pushing at it. If you are too much concerned with hitting inside the baseline, you tend to push the ball. Pushing at the ball is very common at a social or club level of tennis.

Most of the joy of a good tennis stroke lies in being able to swing freely at the ball, and in my experience as a coach, most students—especially in the early stages—are so concerned about getting the ball into the court that they don't give themselves time to develop a natural and powerful swing.

A player who can swing the racket correctly usually succeeds against someone who only pushes at the ball, because a swing generates more power. Everybody on the pro circuit knows how to swing, but Andre Agassi and Monica Seles are exceptional. They swing at everything and, when their game is on, they hit tremendously penetrating balls right at the baseline.

Playing Left and Playing Right

Participants: two players.
Purpose: cutting through learning blocks.

Research into the function of the human brain during the past few decades has shown that the left side of your brain is in charge of the right side of your body, and the right side of your brain is in charge of the left side of your body.

The left brain is associated with your ability to be rational, logical, and methodical; the right side is associated with being intuitive and spontaneous.

Some of the great left-handed players, such as John McEnroe, Martina Navratilova, and Rod Laver developed playing styles that were distinct from right-handed players. McEnroe and Navratilova, particularly, had a touch of genius in their play, an ability to make totally unpredictable shots and maneuvers at unexpected moments during a match. This, I suspect, was due to the influence of the right side of the brain.

As a coach, I have discovered over the years that encouraging right-handed students to practice with their left hands has helped them to become better players.

For example, let us say that one student, Mary, a right-handed player, has a problem hitting a backhand stroke with topspin. At some point, I would suggest to Mary to try doing the same stroke with her left hand, even though she cannot yet do it properly with her right.

In the beginning, Mary finds it very difficult and keeps missing balls. But slowly she develops a sense for the exercise. Then I invite her to switch hands and hit a backhand topspin stroke with her right hand.

Quite often, some dramatic improvements occur. Something clicks on a deep level if you start practicing with your other hand. Your normal side learns from that experience. I have no idea how this happens. I can only observe the effects.

The same thing was noticed during a test with China's top table-tennis players. In a control experiment, one group would do their daily practice routine as usual, using their familiar playing hand. The other group played 50 percent of the time with their familiar hand and 50 percent with the other hand.

An outsider would have said that the second group fooled around for 50 percent of the practice time, doing nothing serious. After two weeks, however, their performances were examined and it was found that the players in the group that practiced with both hands had improved their game by a significantly bigger margin.

Now, the exercise:

If you are right-handed, play ten minutes with the left hand, then ten minutes with your right hand. Repeat three times.

Nick, your partner, feeds the balls to you.

Hit each ball holding your racket with your left hand. Practice hitting a series of forehands, then backhands, then volleys.

It's okay to have fun during this exercise. Feel free to make mistakes because you are again an absolute beginner, playing innocently with this unfamiliar hand. Enjoy the opportunity to be once again in a beginner's space.

When you are ready, switch places and feed balls to Nick.

Red Light, Green Light

Participants: two players.

Purpose: to gain time on the court by improving your decision-making process.

This exercise touches on the complex process of making a split-second decision in a straightforward way.

Nick, your partner, feeds balls to you from the other side of the net.

Your job is to classify each approaching ball as green or red.

Like a traffic light, green stands for go. If you say "Green!" it means that you regard the incoming ball as an easy hit. It means that you feel in charge of the situation, able to attack the ball, and make a shot that will challenge your partner.

Red stands for danger. If you say "Red!" it means that you see this ball as difficult, that you may miss it, that your effort here is only to get the ball safely back over the net.

You shout either "Green!" or "Red!" as soon as it is clear which type of situation you are in, and then perform your shot.

Every ten minutes, switch roles with Nick, feeding balls to each other for one hour.

In the beginning, you will probably shout rather late, just before or even during the moment you hit the ball. You may need to wait until it has bounced before you know what to shout. With practice, you will be able to make the determination at an early stage, while the ball is still flying over the net.

A player who is able to see a situation early with clear

eyes obviously has more time to respond than a player who postpones his decision until the moment of impact.

Another aspect of the exercise is that it encourages you to express and expose the way you perceive different situations on court. If you do this with a coach, he will be able to identify your playing patterns and attitudes more easily.

For example, some of my students would immediately shout "Red!" the moment I presented them with any type of high ball. This enabled me to point out that a short high ball is a totally different situation from a high ball that lands close to the baseline. The short high ball can be green, offering an easy angle to hit a winner.

Watching how a student responds, a coach sees not only how he distinguishes the ball, but how he responds psychologically to green or red situations. For example, I played with one student who, whenever he had a green ball, would simply send it back over the net in a nonaggressive manner. He was happy that the situation did not make him a loser, but he did not use it creatively.

For this student, it was a big change to understand that green situations are opportunities for a wide variety of offensive strokes. As a result, he ended up attacking green balls with enthusiasm.

Each player is different. For example, one of my playing colleagues tends to attack red balls with an attitude of "Okay, you're giving me a red ball, now here's one for you. Let's see how you handle it!"

With time, players start seeing more and more situations as green, which before they could respond to only as red. This in turn makes them better players because a player who is unafraid and offensive has more options than when confined to defensive play. He gives his opponent the feeling that only an extremely well placed ball will put him into red-response mode.

Missing the Ball

Participants: two players.
Purpose: producing fluid and graceful strokes.
Nick, your partner, feeds balls to you from the other end of the court.

In response to each ball, you play a stroke, but you deliberately miss the ball by between five and ten inches.

Let Nick feed you ten balls that you miss deliberately. Then, almost as if by accident, make contact with the eleventh ball.

Hit the next nine balls that Nick feeds to you.

Again, miss the next ten balls deliberately, then again allow your racket to meet the ball for another ten.

Continue the exercise for ten minutes, then switch roles with Nick and feed balls to him.

The chances are that, after missing ten balls deliberately, you will immediately notice a difference in quality from your normal way of hitting a ball.

When most people play tennis, they are so concerned with hitting the ball—with not missing it and looking foolish—that it creates a continuous tension in the way they play the game.

Permission to miss the ball reduces tension and helps you play more effortlessly. Your awareness stays more in your body, with the flow of your movements, than with your concern to get the ball back over the net. This in turn produces fluid and graceful strokes.

This exercise is especially helpful if you are a beginner or someone who has difficulty with a particular stroke.

For example, I remember one student who came to me to learn backhand topspin. He was able to hit backhands only with a slice, and had tried many methods to learn the topspin movement.

I fed him a few balls and asked him to show me his idea of a backhand topspin. In reply, he hit three beautiful backhand slices.

I asked him to show me the topspin movement without ball. He was able to do the movement perfectly. But the moment I presented the ball to him he would slice it. The effort was producing so much tension in his body that he would always do the old and familiar movement.

So I asked him to do this exercise with me: to miss ten balls in a mood of relaxation and enjoyment. I fed balls to both his forehand and backhand.

He became so absorbed by the pleasure of swinging his racket, missing the ball by a few inches, that at one point he accidentally made contact with the ball and hit a perfect backhand topspin.

I said jokingly, "Don't worry, that doesn't count; just keep on missing."

After missing a few more, again by accident he produced another beautiful topspin shot.

After a half hour, the tension in his arms and shoulders had gone, and so had the anxiety in his mind. He was so free from tension and so accustomed to the new swinging movement that he could play backhand topspins deliberately.

The playful attitude that nothing matters, which is an essential ingredient in this kind of exercise, provides a space of relaxation and freedom in which people can learn most easily. It's a Zen paradox: If you let go of results, you end up with the results you want.

Monkey Tennis

Participants: four players in two teams. One team with rackets, one without.

Purpose: enhancing body coordination and team spirit.

One of my favorite ways of entertaining tennis friends is to play a doubles match where one team is using tennis rackets and the other is using only their bare hands.

The pair without rackets catch the oncoming ball and throw it back, while the others respond in the usual way with rackets.

The players without rackets cannot hold onto the ball for more than one or two seconds. After catching the ball they must release it within the time it takes to make a natural throwing movement. They are allowed to take one step forward while throwing the ball.

They serve by throwing from the baseline, from the same position as they would with tennis rackets in their hands.

It's a fun way to practice basic ball skills: your timing, reflexes, coordination, and balance.

I call it monkey tennis because the act of catching the ball and immediately throwing it back reminds me of monkeys. In addition, waiting to receive a fast tennis serve and having to catch it requires a very loose, relaxed body position, rather like a monkey who stands loosely swinging his long arms.

At first glance, it seems obvious that the team without rackets has no chance, but you will be surprised to discover that without rackets you can end up winning the match.

For example, if you are able to catch the ball close to the net you can dink it—just popping it back over the net in a way that nobody can get to it.

If you want to give more chances to the racketless team, you can allow them more time to hold the ball and to make a fake throw before actually releasing it.

This requires alertness and skill from the players with rackets. They have to be on their toes to anticipate the next maneuver.

Speaking personally, it is very exciting to catch a 100-mph serve with one hand. You will feel the lightning responses of the instinctive animal within you and the joy and excitement that comes from doing the unusual and the unpredictable.

There's something in this game that takes you out of your mind, and when you play a lot of tennis—as professionals do—it's a beautiful break from the normal routine. It's fun, social, and exercises your whole body in a different way than a regular tennis game.

Kids love it. It keeps them totally engaged and playing their hearts out. Will the monkeys win or the human beings?

There is an added factor in monkey tennis relating to the development of young, promising tennis players. Recent research indicates that for kids age six to thirteen, it's important to practice different sports, not to focus exclusively on the sport in which they show the most promise.

For example, if a promising young tennis player is also encouraged to play hockey, handball, soccer, basketball, or any other type of ball sport, this will be of more benefit to his or her reflexes than just playing tennis. There is a fine-tuning that happens at this age, through practicing a wide range of athletic and ball skills, that cannot be learned later on.

ADDING FRESHNESS TO YOUR GAME

Often in tennis, the routine of practice and play becomes boring and repetitive and, as a result, your style of play and your attitudes tend to become fixed. These exercises add freshness to your game. They take you out of the usual result-oriented approach and give you new insights as well as opportunities to be playful, spontaneous, and creative on the court.

Inside, you become more alert. Outside, your game becomes sharper. In addition, your chances of slipping into the zone while you play are greatly enhanced.

I Agree with You

A samurai was sitting next to a monk in a ferry, crossing a river. He noticed that although the monk had his eyes closed, he was obviously not sleeping.

Curious, the samurai prodded the monk and asked, "What are you doing?"

The monk opened his eyes and replied, "I am practicing self-awareness."

"How do you do that?" inquired his fellow traveler.

"It is a discipline that requires one to remain fully conscious, no matter what events may occur in one's daily life," the monk responded.

"Pah! Is that all?" scoffed the samurai. "Anybody can do it."

"On the contrary, it is really quite difficult," said the monk.

"Nonsense, just give me a chance to show you," challenged his companion.

"Very well," said the monk. "Simply repeat the phrase, 'I agree with you,' after each statement that I make."

The samurai agreed to do so.

"I am more ancient than these mountains that surround this river," said the mystic.

"I agree with you," said the samurai.

"I have witnessed the rise and fall of many kingdoms."

"I agree with you," said the samurai.

"I lived for many years in the town where you were born."

"I agree with you," said the samurai.

"And your father was a beggar."

"That is a lie!" shouted the samurai, angrily.

"As I was saying," said the monk, "it is really quite difficult to practice self-awareness."

5
Help, I'm Emotional!

Three great tennis players, Jimmy Connors, John McEnroe, and Boris Becker, have all shared one special quality: They have been able to use anger as a way of raising their game, transforming a negative emotion into a positive and creative force.

Connors and McEnroe, especially, reversed the general wisdom that you should not get angry on the court if you want to win—that if you lose your cool you also lose the match. They were fiery characters with a knack for creating situations that gave them permission to become angry and express it, particularly if the score wasn't going their way.

Even on the hallowed greens of Wimbledon, Connors was famous for arguing with linesmen over calls and having lengthy discussions with the chair umpire about anything that was disturbing him. The British public had never seen such behavior and on one celebrated occasion, a BBC television tennis commentator, Peter West, secretly arranged a TV encounter between Connors and one Wimbledon official so that the American could apologize for one of his more memorable outbursts.

But Connors was not impressed by the British attitude toward sporting etiquette. "If I apologize, I have to live with that," he snapped, and walked out of the studio.

McEnroe, too, was involved in hundreds of angry outbursts. The interesting thing about his behavior was that he never directed the anger against himself. This is unusual on the professional circuit. Watch any tournament, live or on TV, and you will see many players being angry with themselves, beating themselves up for making poor shots or tactical errors. McEnroe rarely did that. He directed his anger outward, often toward other people.

Both Connors and McEnroe intuitively understood the value of the emotion we call anger: If you don't fall into the trap of judging it or being ashamed of it or try to hide it, you can see it as an energy source, a fuel that can drive your game to higher levels of performance and greater chances of success.

Of course, this approach has its side effects. Playing against McEnroe, opponents often lost the flow and rhythm of their play as they stood waiting awkwardly during a temper tantrum, embarrassed to be involved in such an emotional scene in front of thousands of people. When play resumed, McEnroe's pent-up frustration had been discharged, but the opponent's had usually increased, leading to erratic play and probable defeat.

For this reason, McEnroe was disliked—even hated—by some players. The same was true for Connors and also for the notorious Ilie Nastase, the Rumanian bad boy of the early seventies who once made the mistake of using these tactics against Roger Taylor, a Scottish player from a rough, working-class background. Taylor lost his rhythm on the court, thanks to a Nastase outburst, but his time came in the locker room afterward, where he punched the Rumanian on the nose, knocking him into the shower.

BECKER'S FIERY TEMPERAMENT

Boris Becker also knows the art of directing emotional energy into his match play. I had the opportunity to observe this firsthand when I played against him in a doubles match in the spring of 1985, just two weeks before he exploded onto the international scene by winning Wimbledon at the age of seventeen.

At that time, people were already noticing Becker, acknowledging him to be a gifted player, but the majority of experts pronounced him too slow in moving around the court—too heavy in his legs—to succeed in any major tournament.

In those days, my partner Stefan and I were considered to be one of the best doubles teams in Germany, and in this interstate championship we were expected to beat Becker and his partner, Jurgen Fassbinder, a Davis Cup player. So when the score reached 5–2 in our favor in the third and final set, we were not particularly surprised. One more game and the match was ours.

As we passed the rival team for the changeover, my partner said to Becker, "Now you see how doubles should be played."

This kind of comment, from older players to newcomers,

happens all the time in sports; especially, I am told, within the hierarchy of a soccer team. It's an effective way of psyching the new, upcoming talent, making them feel inferior, allowing the older players to stay on top of the game a little longer. But in this particular instance, it failed spectacularly.

Becker responded in a way that later became his trademark. With fiery eyes, he walked back onto the court, hit four consecutive winners to bring the score to 5–3, passed us with a series of blistering drives, served a number of aces, ignited his partner to raise his game, and within 15 minutes it was all over. We had lost the set 5–7 and the match as well.

Watching the balls whiz by, I knew there was nothing I could do. I could feel with absolute certainty that this young man was now unstoppable, invincible.

What happened? In a situation like that, most youngsters would have been hurt by Stefan's remark, becoming emotional and then collapsing. Becker also became emotional, but his emotion manifested as anger, which he was able to channel into his game and direct back across the net.

Stefan's remark had awakened a volcano. Without that comment, I am convinced that Becker would not have tapped his dormant energy and we would have won the match. Who knows, maybe the experience even ignited his Wimbledon success as well.

GETTING MAD ON A SATELLITE

When I reflect on my own experience of emotional power, I am reminded of an extraordinary incident that occurred in 1982, while playing a satellite circuit in Yugoslavia, as the region was known then.

Satellite circuits tend to be mean, hungry affairs. These

are the low-profile tennis tournaments where ambitious young players try to pick up enough points to get a better position in the world rankings, thereby gaining access to the big tournaments. Basically, you have to crack the top hundred to stand a chance of entering the Grand Slams.

Anyway, there I was, deep in Yugoslavia, far from the TV cameras, playing a Rumanian Davis Cup player called Dimitri. He was the more experienced player and, sure enough, began to demonstrate his skills by leading the first set 5–2. He was not doing anything special, just returning the ball consistently on the slow clay courts, while I was hitting more errors than winners and getting more and more irritated while doing so.

At 5–2, we changed sides. By then I was so angry with my poor performance that I picked up the heavy iron bench on which I was sitting, raised it above my head and threw it into the middle of the court, shouting at the top of my voice, "This is it! I'm not going to lose one more point to this guy!"

After this outburst, I walked onto the court with the intention of bringing the bench back to the sidelines but was astonished to find that I couldn't lift it even one inch off the ground. How could I possibly have managed to throw it? With difficulty, I managed to drag it to the side of the court so that we could continue playing.

The change in me was drastic. Having gotten rid of my frustration in a single gesture, I went on to win the first set 7–5 and the next set 6–0. I was totally in my energy, playing superb tennis, completely free of tension and self-doubt.

Dimitri, a seasoned player with a great sense of humor—and a bit of a wild man himself—did not report the incident to the tournament officials, and I was doubly fortunate because we were playing without an umpire on a remote court.

Had the match been monitored, I would have been disqualified for unprofessional conduct.

After the match, I talked with Dimitri, who said that although he didn't approve of my behavior, he had to admit that, after the bench-throwing incident, there was nothing he could do except watch me hit countless winners.

By the way, in describing these situations I am not suggesting that you should develop the habit of exploding on court, hurling benches around, or adopting the McEnroe style of throwing temper tantrums during a match. I am simply drawing your attention to the phenomenon of emotional power: how it can either drive or destroy your game.

EVEN SAMPRAS SUFFERS

It is interesting to note that even champions are not always able to use their emotions in healthy ways. In an earlier chapter, I noted how Pete Sampras was able to cry through a difficult situation in the quarterfinals of the 1995 Australian Open, while playing Jim Courier, and go on to win the match. In doing so, he became the darling of the crowd. They loved him, supported him, cheered him.

One year later, during the 1996 Australian Open, Sampras found himself in another difficult situation that did not turn out so well. Sampras was playing the young and upcoming Australian, Mark Philippoussis, and this time the 15,000 capacity crowd was in a feverishly patriotic mood, loudly supporting Philippoussis, hoping that he would recapture the golden days when great Australian players like Rod Laver and Roy Emerson dominated the world tennis scene.

Watching this game, I could feel that Sampras was unable to move into his usual high gear. He seemed to be playing politely, going through the motions, as if half-dead. He was trying different strategies, trying to get Philippoussis to make mistakes, but I could see from his face that his heart was not in it.

At that time, Sampras was winning almost everything on the pro circuit, so what was happening on this occasion? My feeling is that the American was emotionally poisoned inside. He couldn't believe that this audience, which only a year ago had given him a standing ovation, had now totally abandoned him.

He was hurt, disappointed, but playing it cool, trying not to show anything. As a result, the unexpressed energy was eating him up. His performance was not real. He did not know how to translate his hurt into a healthy anger against this fickle crowd—an anger that would have reignited his energy and brought him back into the match.

I also suspect that Sampras was not able to understand what he was feeling. It would have been embarrassing for the American to admit—even to himself—that his performance could be affected by something so superficial as not being appreciated, as playing before a crowd that was cheering only for the other player.

It is worth noting that Sampras and Philippoussis are both of Greek origin, and that the American had already demonstrated a brotherly feeling toward the Australian at the 1995 U.S. Open. After beating Philippoussis in a close match, Sampras became the first top player to state publicly that Philippoussis had the potential to be a world star. This probably made the situation more difficult for Sampras as he sagged to defeat under the hot Australian sun, because he felt an obligation to be nice to his opponent.

One way out for the American would have been to use a little theater, to have done something playful or amusing, thereby winning support from members of the audience—and there are a few in every crowd—who might be feeling uncomfortable about the partisan pressure.

TURNING ENERGY AROUND

By way of contrast, I am reminded of the Boris Becker–Andre Agassi semifinal in the 1995 Wimbledon tournament, where Becker lost the first set 6–1 and was trailing 4–1 in the second set. The British spectators were clearly behind Agassi, who was playing spectacularly entertaining tennis.

Becker did not go down the tunnel of negative emotion that captured Sampras in his match against Philippoussis. Instead, he found a way to turn the crowd around. When he finally managed to break Agassi's serve for the first time to make the score 2–4, he spontaneously put on a show, raising his arms and facing the crowd as if he had won the whole match, bowing to all four sides of the court.

Even though it was a small victory, just a single game, he was saying to the crowd, "Okay, I'm still alive in this contest and now it's time for you to applaud me!" The crowd loved it and responded with huge applause. Even Agassi had to smile at his opponent's guts and spirit.

Becker got emotionally fueled by the appreciation of the audience and went on to play a superb match, winning in four sets. He had found a way to turn the energy around. In that moment, at least, he was a true man of Zen.

DON'T POSTPONE EMOTIONS

The bottom line with emotion on a tennis court is: If you do not recognize it and find a way of releasing it, the unexpressed energy is going to turn against you and eat you alive, sucking your vitality, making you collapse.

Most people have had this kind of experience at some point in their lives, becoming so affected emotionally that they don't know what to say anymore. They become tongue-tied, as if all intelligence has left their brains, as if they no longer have a will of their own. They feel as if all energy has suddenly drained out of their bodies.

These side effects happen when you do not know, cannot accept, or cannot express what you are feeling. Such is our lack of experience in dealing with these powerful energies that several hours may pass before clarity arises and you realize that you were angry, sad, or hurt. But if this happens on the tennis court, by the time you realize what has happened, it's too late. You are already in the locker room and the match is lost.

As a Zen player, you can't afford the luxury of postponing your emotions. Of course, it is always helpful to look back on a difficult situation and realize what was happening to you—"emotion recollected in tranquillity," as the English poet Wordsworth put it. This will make it easier next time to understand your feelings as they arise. Nevertheless, as a sporting warrior, looking back is rather like attending your own autopsy. As far as combat is concerned, your head has already been chopped off.

Being able to deal with your emotions immediately, as they occur, makes you more successful as a player. In a match, you have to be full of energy, vitally alive. You can't afford to be drained, distracted, or confused.

MENTAL TOUGHNESS

Strangely enough, there is very little guidance or training available to help players deal creatively with this important aspect of their game. The most popular solution is to try to control emotions, and this approach has been turned into a dramatic art by the model of mental toughness that is currently popular among some professionals.

Mental toughness is a complex affair, but if I needed to state its basic principle in a single sentence, I'd say it is a method through which a player can create his desired mental and emotional state on the tennis court—a bit like an actor on a stage.

This approach begins from the perspective that body and mind are a single organism. It teaches a certain ritual of repetitive body movements that can send a continuous message to the mind that everything is under control.

In your practice sessions, you learn a drill: After each point, regardless of whether you won or lost, act in a confident manner, turn away from the net with your head up, look at the strings of your racket, walk assertively back to the baseline, get ready for the next point . . .

You do this hundreds of times, so that during a match your ritual continues to send a positive message. Using specific and repetitive body gestures between points, regardless of whether you are winning or losing, you maintain a confident mental attitude.

The mental toughness approach says you cannot control your opponent, you cannot control the score, but you can control your own attitude, behavior, and emotions. After missing a volley you might not feel confident, but at least you can walk confidently. Just like a good actor, make it up as you go along. "Fake it until you make it," was the advice of one trainer.

TENNIS: ONLY A MIND GAME?

This approach can help in terms of a player's performance, but it is also easy to give too much credit to the mental side. These days, it has become almost conventional wisdom among many tennis experts that all the leading players have all the shots, and therefore the only difference lies in their mental strength.

I disagree. It's true that most players are highly trained athletes, but over the past ten years, one can easily note significant stroke weaknesses among famous world-class players: Connors's serve, Borg's volley, Edberg's forehand, Sabatini's serve, Seles' nonexistent volley, are all technical defects.

Today, it is recognized that Goran Ivanisevic has the world's best serve, shooting an incredible number of aces, but still he can't seem to win a major title. My feeling is that his poor performance in the grand slams is not caused solely by a lack of mental toughness. In the first place, he loses his mental composure, getting angry and frustrated, because of his defective technique and strategic errors on the court.

Looking at it another way, both Pete Sampras and Ivanisevic have great serves. But there is a major difference in what these two players do with the ball once an opponent manages to return it over the net. Sampras has a killer volley and a repertoire of other intelligent responses, whereas Ivanisevic usually runs into trouble, as if surprised that anyone could possibly return his serve. The open question is: What does Ivanisevic need, a better mental game, or more variety in his strokes? I'd say he could benefit from both.

To me, mental toughness is something of a superficial technique. It does not reach deep enough. It does not help you deal with your emotions. It simply offers a way to bypass them—and personally, I don't think that ignoring or suppressing emotions can work for very long.

DEFEAT: FACING THE UNAVOIDABLE

There is a basic law of competition that every professional has to face: in a singles tournament only one player wins. Everyone else loses. This means that, in a Grand Slam contest where 128 players enter the first round, there are going to be 127 losers. In the first round alone, half of the players are finished. By the third morning of the tournament, 64 people wake up not being part of the singles competition anymore.

Everybody who is on the pro circuit knows that players are deeply affected by the possibility of not making it through the first round of a Grand Slam. These are the tournaments they live for, train for, pray for. These are the ultimate tests to body, mind and spirit. This is where you can be catapulted into the glare of the television lights, where stars are created and legends are born, but only if you win, only if you can make it through the opening rounds.

During the Australian Open in 1996, I watched several first-round matches, walking from one court to another, and I did not come across a single player who was smiling or in a mood of relaxed enjoyment. That's an indication of how tight and tense the players are in the early stages of a big tournament.

Only if they survive the first and second rounds will something inside relax, because then they know they haven't been an embarrassment to themselves. Then at least they can look back and say, "Oh, I made it to the third round of a Grand Slam," or, better yet, "I made it through two rounds of the U.S. Open and then lost to Agassi. He was in great form that year."

This, then, is the kind of pressure under which players enter a major tournament. I'm not saying mental toughness can't help, but it doesn't alter the brutal mathematics of competition. Even if you and your opponent are both trained in being mentally tough, one of you is going to win and one is going to lose.

In my experience, when players find themselves on the losing side of a game, they have a strong need to release feelings of frustration, disappointment, embarrassment, or anger, but this is not encouraged. Instead, they train themselves to contain their feelings, so there is no outlet for the strong emotions that may now be raging beneath a mask of self-control.

CORE ISSUES

In other words, this approach does not deal with the core issues that players have to confront when they walk off the court in defeat, including—perhaps the worst nightmare of all—the sensation of having let your country down and seeing this reflected in the headlines of your national newspapers.

Michael Stich, one of the most gifted players to come out

of Germany, got a taste of this bitter medicine a few years ago when he was elevated to number two in the world rankings. In minor tournaments he did consistently well, but in the Grand Slams there was a period when he lost repeatedly in the opening rounds. As a result, he received a terrible lashing from the German press and this in turn put him under even greater pressure when he entered the next big tournament.

Issues like embarrassment and disgrace are very real for professional players. They don't talk about it, but it can affect them so badly that they are unable even to play normal shots, let alone spectacular winners. Their arms become heavy—the so-called iron arm syndrome—so that they can hardly lift their rackets.

We are dealing with powerful psychological mechanisms that have deep roots in our psyche. On a surface level, little tricks can be used to temporarily persuade the mind that everything is okay, but the real transformative work has to go much deeper.

THE NEED FOR INNER WORK

In my view, the first and most important step for a player who has become emotional is to be aware of what is happening to him. It may sound easy and overly simplistic, but our cultural and social environment has been so condemnatory of emotion that it is really quite difficult to honestly recognize an emotion when it surfaces.

This is where the coach's input can be crucial. If a player has lost a match and in doing so has encountered a negative or traumatic experience, then he needs to do inner work. He needs support to complete what has happened on the court.

He needs to replay that match, to relive it and, with the help of a coach, gain understanding of what took place in his mind and in his feelings.

Unfortunately, the majority of the coaches deal with their players only on a technical level. They are not equipped to deal with inner processes. Feedback tends to remain on the level of "Next time you have a match point, try to get your first serve in and don't take such a big risk." That's the guidance players usually hear from coaches in the dressing room.

I'm not saying that every player needs a consulting psychologist. I am saying running over our feelings and trying to push them away will serve only to give them additional strength in the hidden parts of our minds, which guarantees that they will resurface like unfriendly ghosts at the very moment when we least wish to see them—namely, when the pressure starts to mount in the next tournament.

There are techniques you can use to express and release unwanted emotions, both on and off the court. Before any of these techniques can work, you need to develop the knack of recognizing and acknowledging what you are feeling, in the very moment that you are feeling it.

This takes a lot of self-awareness. It requires a Zen approach to tennis, because in order to accept what you are feeling, you need to be able to switch your focus from the outer reality—the match, the score, winning, and losing—to your inner reality. It is this switch that allows you to gain distance and detachment from your emotions while they are happening.

The ability to change focus from outer to inner reality is acquired through the practice of meditation. The meditator, by penetrating deeply into his own inner reality, comes to know that he is not his feelings, that he can be a witness to all the turmoil that his emotions are creating. From this inner space, it becomes much easier to be aware of emotional energy as it arises and to deal with it in a direct and creative manner.

Let's See What Happens

A poor farmer lived with his son in a remote part of the countryside. One day, the son came home from a nearby village filled with happiness and exclaimed, "Father, it is wonderful! I have met a beautiful young woman and she loves me! We can be married. She can come and live with us and take care of you in your old age."

"Let's see what happens," said the farmer.

The son thought his father's response very odd, but said nothing about it.

A few days later, the son came home tortured with despair. "Alas, how unlucky I am!" he exclaimed. "This young woman is the daughter of the bandit chief who every year takes half of our crops. He will surely kill me if he discovers that I want to marry his daughter."

"Let's see what happens," said the farmer. Again, the son found his father's response very puzzling.

One week passed. Then the son came home with a radiant expression on his face. "What great good fortune!" he cried. "My lover has confessed every-thing to her father. He has agreed to the marriage and will no longer steal our crops! We will become rich!"

"Let's see what happens," said his father.

A few weeks later, government troops swept through the land. The son came home weeping. "Alas! How unfortunate I am!" he cried. "The troops have attacked the bandit chief's stronghold and killed everyone. My beloved is dead!"

"Let's see what happens," said the father.

Next day, the young woman appeared at their door, seeking refuge after escaping from the troops. Exhausted, she fell into her lover's arms.

The son was about to express his good fortune, when he looked at his father and together they said, "Let's see what happens."

6
Transforming
Emotional Energy

Emotions are enemies only when you do not give them permission to exist. Once you have the ability to recognize and accept them, they not only become your friends, they become powerful sources of vitality and energy that can be directed into your game, enhancing your level of play and skill.

The exercises in this chapter are designed to help you become familiar with your emotions and help you express and release the energy they contain. In addition, the chapter includes meditation techniques that help you reach a point of centeredness within yourself that will enable you to disidentify from your emotions while they are occurring.

When you are identified with a feeling, such as anger, it means that you are so close to the anger that it is consuming you, ruling you, and controlling you. In a sense, you are the anger. There is no distinction between the emotion and your sense of self. For most people, when anger or some other powerful emotion arises, it takes over, shutting out the normal, rational processes of the conscious mind. This loss of control is why society teaches people to suppress such feelings, fearing the power they contain.

However, it is possible to find a point of centeredness within yourself where, even while an emotion is raging, you can remain unidentified with it. You can be a spectator, standing at the center of the cyclone that is whirling around you. You can feel the anger, you can allow the energy of this emotion to pass through you, but you are not swept away by it.

Once you have had even a small taste of disidentification, any fear that you may have of your own emotions begins to lose its grip. You will know that this feeling, this anger, is not really you, and you will also know that it is not going to destroy you. You have an inner strength that will allow you to accept the emotion instead of trying to push it away. This is the gift that meditation can bring to the Zennis player.

One of the ways in which people tend to dismiss emotions is to say that they are childish. This is true in the sense that very young children often have permission to be uninhibited and spontaneous in the expression of their feelings. They have not yet been trained in the ways of social manners and correct behavior.

To be familiar with your emotions, it can be helpful to become, for a little while, a small child again, and this is what I invite you to do in the first exercises of this chapter. These exercises are not difficult. In fact, they are very simple, but your adult mind may rebel against them at first, precisely because they seem to be childish. You, the cool tennis player, the one who always has everything under control, behaving like a child? Forget it!

Nevertheless, I encourage you to put aside such adult notions for a few minutes and indulge in the carefree, irresponsible, spontaneous world of a six-year-old. You will be surprised at how much vitality and energy it can release. If you can manage to find a suitable place where you can make noise and be undisturbed, then no one will ever know your secret. Try it and see.

OFF-COURT EXERCISES

The Stubborn Child

The purpose of this exercise is to give you a chance to express your emotional negativity. Often, especially in childhood, or as adults when receiving orders from a person in authority, we are not allowed to express our spontaneous negative reaction to those orders. We are not allowed to say no.

Instead, we have to eat it, swallow it. The energy is held in, and when energy is held in, it kills our vitality and our enthusiasm for life. This exercise is an opportunity to release some of that pent-up energy.

Find a space where you will not be disturbed, and imagine that you are a small child, between four and seven years old. Your father or mother has just ordered you to do something—go to your room, clean up your mess, stay indoors, do your homework, eat your food—and you do not want to do this.

Fully express saying no, with your voice, your face, and your body.

Raise your voice, furrow your brow, clench your fists, stamp your feet, shake your head, and say loudly, "No! No! No!" Just like a stubborn child. Or, if you prefer, "No, I won't!"

Make sure you stamp firmly on the floor with your heels.

Don't worry if the adult part of your mind is telling you that this is silly. Pay no attention. Put your total energy into the exercise. Get so lost into it that you actually become the stubborn child; this time your parents have no power to make you do anything that you do not want to do. This time your no means exactly that: No!

Do this for a few minutes. You will feel fresh energy moving in your body. You will feel more alive and vital, and you may end up having a good laugh.

On a practical note: if you do this exercise at home, and do not have a soundproof cellar or room, the best way to prevent others from hearing you and possibly disturbing you is to play loud music during the exercise. This will drown out your vocal expression.

The Helpless Child

This exercise takes you directly to the place that most people spend their whole lives trying to avoid: the state of complete collapse, giving in to the feeling of inadequacy, an inability to cope or to achieve anything—in short, the feeling of utter failure.

This exercise is a little more difficult. It takes courage, even when you are alone, but it is extremely powerful if you can manage it. Like the previous exercise, it may seem a bit off the wall to your adult, sophisticated mind, but just try it and see the effect.

Imagine that you have just experienced a spectacularly embarrassing incident. For example, you were the top seed in the U.S. Open and you just lost in straight sets in the first round. Or you missed a simple volley at match point in the final of the Davis Cup and as a result your country has lost the trophy.

Give space to all the feelings that this disastrous experience evokes in you, but respond to them as a child would, not as an adult. Find a table, bench, or bed, crawl under it and curl up like a little baby. You may wish to take a teddy bear with you, or you may want to suck your thumb.

As in the previous exercise, engage your entire body in the experience—involve your voice, your face, your arms, your legs.

Begin to make mewling or whining noises, as a baby would do when it has been left alone too long. You can support this feeling by making a gentle rocking motion with your body, closing your eyes, sucking your thumb, and perhaps saying a few words like, "I'm sorry, Mommy."

Allow yourself to experience the feeling that there's nothing you can do, and nothing you do is ever going to work. Whatever expectations your parents have of you, you will never manage to live up to them. Feel the hopelessness and despair, feel it and express it as a small child would.

Don't be in a hurry. Give yourself a chance so that these feelings can take over. Give full permission to this neglected space, acknowledging the helplessness within. We are often taught to be stoic and accept loss and defeat with a stiff upper lip. This exercise can allow you to tap into the sadness you felt over past losses and let it go. There can be a feeling of tremendous relief in allowing yourself to feel what has been suppressed and hidden for so many years.

If you are wondering how this can help your tennis game, you may wish to consider the Japanese samurai way of life. The best warriors, the ones who had the greatest chance of being victorious, were those who had already explored and experienced the very thing they were facing on the field of battle: the fear of death. Through meditation, they had already moved into an inner, deathlike experience and were therefore free from the grip of fear.

For an athlete who participates in competition, one of the greatest fears is that of being an utter failure. The athlete who has already moved into this experience, who has made friends with this disowned energy, will be less ruled by such fears during a match than one who is trying to push such fears away. They will have less grip over you. You will not take them so seriously.

There are many variations to these two child-oriented exercises. For example, you can experiment with simply playing as a child: running around the room, screaming, shouting, jumping, rolling on the floor like a six-year-old. This will provoke many feelings inside, not only negative but also positive. And if you can find someone to play with you in the same spirit, this will be a powerful experience for you both.

Speaking Gibberish

This is a simple yet powerful method of releasing mental tension. It can be especially helpful just before an important match, when you are driving yourself crazy thinking about all the possible strokes and strategies you may need against this particular opponent: how he's going to play, what his strengths are, what you have to watch out for, etc., etc.

This exercise is based on a Sufi technique for clearing the mind as a prelude to devotion or meditation. It originated with a Sufi mystic called Jabbar, and consequently became known as *gibberish*.

Find a safe place where you will not be disturbed, and instead of listening to your mind's endless stream of suggestions—which, if they continue long enough, are bound to start contradicting each other—you can free your mental energy in a creative and energizing way.

Start talking to yourself in an unknown or invented language. Make sounds like Russian, Chinese, German, Martian—any kind of language is okay as long as it does not make sense to you.

For best results, you need to speak loudly, urgently, and forcefully, almost as if you are mad or possessed. Just let the sounds pour out of your mouth in a continuous flood.

Use your whole body to support what you are saying. Make dramatic gestures. Stand up, walk around. If you find it helpful, imagine you are addressing the Annual Galactic Alien Sports Conference on Mars or Jupiter.

You may find yourself getting angry, happy, sad, or irritable. Welcome the emotion, whatever it is, and express the feeling through the gibberish that comes out of your mouth.

Totality is the name of the game. The more wholeheartedly you do the exercise, the greater the benefits will be.

Do this for five to ten minutes, then sit quietly for a few minutes, with your eyes closed, enjoying the sense of release and peace that follows this chaotic form of expression.

ON-COURT EXERCISES

Whatever methods you employ to release and express feelings on the court need to be within the rules of the game and the conduct of sportsmanship. For example, you cannot beat your racket to a pulp. You cannot hit a ball way over the fence in a rage. You cannot shout at your opponent. You are not supposed to abuse the officials.

But the rules do give some space for self-expression while playing, during the twenty-five-second gap between points, and in the sixty-second gap during the changeover after every two games.

Here are seven suggestions. The first two exercises are practiced on the bench, while changing sides. The next two can be practiced while playing. The last three can be done in the short gaps between points.

Breathing on the Bench

The purpose of this exercise is to help you center yourself, saying "Yes" to whatever you are feeling, and using the breath to move the energy through your body.

At the changeover, sit comfortably with a straight back, allowing your belly to be relaxed and big. Do not try to hold it in. Close your eyes.

As you sit, begin by observing how far your breath reaches inside. Notice if it is only in the upper chest. Gently bring your breathing down into your belly, so it becomes deep and slow. The more you can relax and reach the belly area, the longer your out breath will take. Eventually the out breath takes three times longer than the in breath.

If you notice any tension in your body, relax it consciously, especially in the shoulders.

The Towel Meditation

This exercise helps you to stay focused on yourself and avoid distractions while playing a match. During the changeover period, sit on your bench and drape a towel over your head so that it covers your face. Your eyes should be half open; keep them unfocused.

This may look odd, but Arthur Ashe did it on center court during the 1975 Wimbledon final and beat Jimmy Connors, the favorite. He was the first player to meditate on court during a major tournament.

Breathe slowly and deeply into your belly. Use this period to get in touch with your underlying feelings and emotions. This is your only opportunity during the match to be silent and check inside yourself to see what exactly is going on.

Maybe you will discover a negative feeling such as the fear of failure. Then you can acknowledge to yourself, "Yes, I'm afraid of failing in this match." This provides an authentic connection with your emotions and your energy, and my experience is that once you get in touch with an emotion in an authentic way, it changes and disappears.

Do not try to counter a negative thought with a positive one, as many coaches suggest. This will keep you disconnected from your energy. It is your acknowledgment of what is happening in the moment that is the key.

Making Sounds

This is a potent method of releasing frustration and anger. As you hit the ball, accompany your action with a loud grunt—"Ugh!" or "Hah!"—expelling the air forcefully out of your lungs as you do so. This ensures that you will not suppress any energy and permit it to become negative, turning against yourself.

Another benefit of this exercise is that when you make a sound with each stroke it improves your rhythm of play. You become your own drumbeat.

Hitting the Ball Harder

Giving yourself permission to hit at full strength will release pent-up frustration and aggression. Hit the ball very hard, two or three times, down the middle of the court. This technique was used by Bjorn Borg when a match was not going well. The chances are that these shots will not be as accurate as your normal play, so don't aim for the corners, otherwise you will lose too many points.

Tensing Your Hands

It sounds paradoxical, but one way to become more relaxed is to make a conscious effort to be as tense as possible. This is a technique based on progressive muscle relaxation.

Your hands get easily affected by nervousness and can become shaky and sweaty, making precision strokes difficult to execute. This exercise helps you to reduce tension in your hands and regain a fluid sense of play.

Grip the handle of your tennis racket with both hands and press as hard as you can, using all your muscles. Do this three times for three seconds each time, as if you are trying to squeeze juice out of the racket handle. Take a deep breath, exhale, and keep on playing.

Stamping Your Feet

In the breaks between points, stamp your feet. This simple technique will help to ground the energy that is building inside you and will also give you the feeling that it is okay to be angry, that you have a right to be angry in this moment.

Tensing Your Whole Body

This exercise is similar to gripping the racket, but is done with your whole body.

Take a deep breath and hold the air in. As you do so, tense every muscle in your body, especially those in your hands and face. Hold your breath and the tension for as long as you can, then let go. Repeat this three times.

BASIC MEDITATION TECHNIQUES

Meditation is one of the most essential aspects of Zennis. It is the art of creating inner silence, the art of disidentifying from whatever thoughts and feelings we are experiencing at any given moment.

If the Zennis player wishes to experience the bliss of playing in the zone, free from self-doubt and anxiety, moving around the court in a natural and spontaneous way, then meditation is a must.

Meditation has a long history, especially in Eastern countries like India, Tibet, China, and Japan. The spiritual paths that developed in these countries, such as Taoism, Hinduism, and Buddhism, as well as spiritual practices such as Yoga, Tantra, and Zen, have created hundreds of different meditation methods.

How to find the right technique? Since meditation is not a spectator sport, you cannot tell by watching someone else meditate. You will need to explore and experiment. When you find a technique that creates a silent space within, this is the right method for you.

In fact, the function of all meditations is the same: to experience inner silence and peace, to know yourself as pure consciousness, as a flame of awareness that is beyond the body-mind mechanism.

From this space you can see at firsthand that you are not your body, you are not your thoughts, you are not your feelings. You experience disidentification from all the things that you normally consider yourself to be.

This experience happens when the mind is silent, when the thinking process has temporarily ceased, when you are feeling relaxed, at home in yourself, accepting yourself exactly the way you are.

When you have grasped the basic principles, you can even devise your own methods. Here are two basic approaches to meditation: traditional sitting meditations and modern, active meditations.

TRADITIONAL SITTING MEDITATIONS

Vipassana

Gautama Buddha, as many people know, was a prince who lived in Northern India approximately 2,500 years ago. At the age of 33, he renounced his kingdom in order to pursue a spiritual quest. For many years he practiced severe austerities, including fasting, but in the end gave up asceticism, seeing that it had not brought him any closer to self-illumination.

Instead, he practiced what came to be known as Vipassana, the meditation method that led to his enlightenment and later became the primary method for Buddha's followers.

You are welcome to experiment with Vipassana, as follows:

Wearing loose clothing, sit in a comfortable position on a cushion or meditation stool. If this is difficult, you can also use a chair. Keep your spine erect, but let your body be relaxed. In particular, let your belly be loose, with no constricting belt or elastic.

Be comfortable. Your sitting position should not create stress or tension in your body.

Let your hands rest in your lap.

Close your eyes.

When you feel settled, focus your attention on the movement of your breath as it passes in and out of your body.

This can be done in two ways:

You can focus on the sensation in your nose, feeling the cool air entering through your nostrils as you inhale, feeling the warmer air leaving through your nostrils as you exhale.

Or, if it is easier, you can focus on the rise and fall of your belly as you inhale and exhale.

When I say "focus your attention," I do not mean that you should concentrate hard on these sensations, since this effort will make you tense. It is, rather, an attitude of effortless awareness, just noticing the sensations in a relaxed but alert way as they occur in your body.

You will also notice that your attention wanders away from your breathing. You may find yourself distracted by a noise in the neighborhood or by physical sensations in your body—an itch or an ache—or by a thought arising in your mind.

This will happen many times. Each time it happens, remember that you are supposed to be watching your breathing, and bring your attention back to the exercise.

After a while, say twenty to thirty minutes, your body will probably become stiff. This is a sign that it is time to begin the second stage of the meditation. Slowly open your eyes, stand up, and begin to walk very slowly in a circle, eyes looking down toward the ground about three feet ahead of you. Your hands are gently clasped in front of your body, resting against your belly.

Walk meditatively in this way for about ten minutes, all the while focusing your attention on your breathing. You may never have walked in this slow, conscious way before, and it can be a powerful experience.

When you are ready, return to the sitting position and close your eyes.

I suggest that you practice Vipassana for one hour: twenty-five minutes sitting, ten minutes walking, twenty-five minutes sitting.

You can do this meditation indoors or outdoors, alone or

with a group of other meditators. It is essentially a Buddhist meditation, and there may be a group near you that can guide you in regular practice.

Zazen

Bodhidharma, the first patriarch of Zen, brought Gautama Buddha's message of meditation from India to China. However, after a historic encounter at the border with Emperor Wu, he decided not to enter the country. Instead, he sat for nine years in a cave, looking at a wall.

This was Bodhidharma's way of saying that people were not yet ready to listen to him or understand him. In these nine years, he turned wall-watching into a fine art for those seekers who gathered to be with him and thereby created Zazen.

In Zazen, you sit with eyes open, facing a plain white wall.

You breathe normally. Instead of watching the movement of your breath, you watch your mind. This is Bodhidharma's essential teaching: spiritual liberation, or enlightenment, is attained through the practice of beholding the mind. Nothing more is necessary.

As you sit, doing nothing, looking at the wall, you simply watch the whole spectrum of thoughts and feelings as they arise within you.

Zazen has, over the centuries, become a ritualized affair, especially when it is performed as a meditation retreat in a Zen monastery. The day begins early, at 5:30 A.M., with 108 bows or prostrations, with which you salute your buddha nature. This is followed by sessions of chanting, wall-watching, slow walking, and also contemplating Zen koans.

A koan is a question that is essentially insoluble. The purpose of a koan is to bring your mind to such a point of intense, focused effort—on a question that has no answer—that, at a certain point, your thinking process gives up the struggle and your mind relaxes, opening the way to a sudden and profound experience of no mind.

Classic Zen koans include:

° What is the sound of one hand clapping?
° Where was the moon before there was time?
° How many lives does a cat have?

If you are attracted to Zazen and would like a few Zennis koans on which your mind can chew while you are watching the wall, I can offer you the following:

° Where was the Grand Slam before it was created?
° How can I hit an ace without hitting an ace?
° Is the tennis ball inside or outside my mind?
° Who is it that wins?
° Who is it that loses?
° What was Steffi Graf's name before she was born?
° What is the ultimate score?

If you think you have found the answer, you haven't chewed long enough. The revelation, when it comes, is beyond knowledge.

ACTIVE MEDITATIONS

Active meditation techniques are recent developments, designed to deal with the fact that modern man is a more up-tight, stressed-out, hyperactive creature than the people who meditated with Gautama Buddha or Bodhidharma.

It is really quite difficult for twentieth-century human beings to sit and do nothing. Even on a day off, we usually manage to complete a full schedule of activities: watching TV, reading a newspaper, surfing the web, chatting on the telephone. There is even a social phenomenon known as leisure-time stress caused by pressure of events during days off. Doing nothing, really doing nothing, tends to make us feel restless, uneasy, and bored.

Teachers of meditation who understand the modern predicament have created active techniques to help release mental and physical tension before moving into silence and stillness.

The following two meditation techniques were created by Osho, an Indian mystic who lived between 1931 and 1990. For both meditations, I recommend using specially created music tapes that will help you participate fully in the techniques and also provide timing for each stage (see Endnotes).

Dynamic Meditation

This meditation is best done in the early morning.

It has five stages and lasts one hour. It is very energetic and is not recommended for people who have severe medical disabilities such as heart problems.

The meditation is done standing.

It is best to keep your eyes closed throughout the meditation. You may even wish to use a blindfold.

Stage one (ten minutes): Begin with deep, fast, rapid breathing through your nose, emphasizing the exhale. Use your whole body to help you breathe as deeply and strongly as possible. Let the breathing be chaotic—in other words do not fall into a fixed pattern of breathing. The chaotic breathing will stir up all kinds of feelings inside you. You will not hyperventilate if you breathe through your nose, not your mouth.

Stage two (ten minutes): Express everything that has been provoked by the breathing. Scream, shout, laugh, cry, be angry, be sad, be joyful—let it all out. If you do not have a soundproof space that permits you to scream, you can do this stage silently, expressing your feelings by punching the air, hitting a cushion, throwing your arms and legs around in a chaotic way, making all kinds of facial expressions, and so on. Let yourself go completely.

Stage three (ten minutes): Jump in the air with your arms raised above your head, shouting the mantra, "Hoo!" Each time you jump, make sure you land with flat feet, so that your heels hit the ground. This jumping movement acts as a hammer on your sex center, awakening vital energy that spreads through your body. Exhaust yourself in this stage of the meditation.

Stage four (fifteen minutes): Stop. Freeze in one position and hold it without moving. Simply be a witness to everything that is happening inside you, both in your physical body and in your mind. Just let everything be as it is.

Stage five (fifteen minutes): Complete the meditation with free-form dancing, celebrating the energy that has been awakened within you.

Kundalini Meditation

This meditation also lasts one hour and is gentler than Dynamic Meditation.

It has four stages, each lasting fifteen minutes.

Stage one: In a standing position, shake your body. Shake your hands, arms, head, torso, hips, legs. Shake everything. Be loose. Do not make muscular effort to shake. Rather, allow the shaking to happen. Let it take you over. Become the shaking.

Stage two: Dance freely in any manner that you wish. Express the energy that has been awakened in your body through the shaking.

Stage three: Sit or stand quietly, with closed eyes.

Stage four: Lie down on the floor, on your back, and relax completely. Simply be a passive witness to everything that is happening, inside and out.

GRASPING THE BASIC PRINCIPLE

The understanding inherent in these meditations, and, indeed, in all forms of active meditation, is that we need to free ourselves of mental and physical tension if we wish to relax into silence. Otherwise, deep relaxation is difficult, if not impossible. Relaxation is one of those elusive states that cannot be achieved through effort. If we try to do it, if we make efforts to relax, we succeed only in making ourselves more tense.

Active meditation says forget all about relaxation. Instead, move to the opposite polarity. Throw yourself into total activity, total effort, awakening and expressing the energy in your body. Then relaxation happens effortlessly, by it-self, and meditation becomes simple and easy.

Once you have grasped this principle, you may like to create your own active techniques.

DANCING

Dancing is one of the best ways of freeing yourself of ten-sion. Just put on your favorite music and dance wildly, freely, totally, for about thirty minutes, then sit or lie down with your eyes closed, relax, and meditate for another thirty minutes.

RUNNING

Maybe you enjoy running. Run until you feel exhausted, and then sit or lie down, close your eyes, and go inside. This is an excellent method to practice in nature, along a shore-line or in a forest.

PLAYING WITH A BALL MACHINE

On a tennis court, you can experiment with playing in-tensely with a ball machine. Play 100 balls each on your fore-hand and backhand. This will exhaust you. Then, with your heart pumping, sit down on a chair or bench and close your eyes for five minutes, doing nothing. Collect the balls, fill up the machine, and repeat the exercise two or three times.

Any activity that helps you to become energized, that helps you to express and release your energy, will bring you to a point where you can meditate. Once you can meditate, you are on the path of Zen.

The Perfect Guru

*A spiritual seeker set off with a band of friends in
search of a guru. He came across many teachers,
many mystics, many wise men, but he rejected them
all, not wishing to stay even when some of his friends
remained behind to be initiated as disciples. "I can
see their weaknesses, their frailties," he objected. "I
am in search of the perfect guru." He traveled on for
many years until all his friends had left him.*

*Finally, he arrived at a remote cave, deep in the
Himalayas, wherein sat an impressive-looking man
with piercing eyes, a long white beard, and a magnif-
icent aura of radiance around his head and shoulders.*

*"At last, I have found you!" cried the seeker.
"You are the perfect guru. Please initiate me immediately.*

*"I cannot do that," replied the guru, "because I
am looking for the perfect disciple."*

7
The Four Demons:
Perfectionism, Self-Criticism, Boredom, and Expectation

Every Grand Slam contains a hundred stories, and it is possible to find examples for all the issues that I address in this book in a single major tournament. Such incidents are happening all the time, and although I use examples mainly from the Grand Slams of 1995 and 1996 when this book was being written, you can find similar examples by watching any of the current tournaments.

One of the most interesting contests in the '96 French Open was a match that many people missed. It took place early in the tournament, in the second round, between Pete Sampras, the number-one seed, and Sergi Bruguera, the clay court specialist from Spain. The match was very close, stretching Sampras to five sets. Since Andre Agassi lost in the same round, both results were greeted with surprise by the media. One top seed had crashed, and another seemed to be struggling.

Neither result was really surprising. Agassi had been injured and had practiced very little for the tournament. The real surprise would have been if Agassi had done well. Sampras, meanwhile, was taking on the man who had won Paris in '93 and '94. They were meeting in an early round because Bruguera had slipped in the world rankings and was therefore not seeded. In terms of class and style, the Sampras-Bruguera encounter was worthy of a tournament final.

At the end of a skillful and artistic match, a victorious Sampras walked off the court in happy mood. You could see that he was deeply satisfied with his performance. When asked by the media how he rated the match in his already-exceptional career, Sampras replied, "That was maybe my best clay court match so far."

I wondered about that remark, because in terms of hard statistics, it was not an impressive performance by the champion. Sampras had won the first two sets quite convincingly at 6–4 and 6–3 but lost the third set 6–7 and seemed to throw away the fourth set 2–6, committing many unforced errors. He eventually rescued the match in the fifth and final set. From total points played, Sampras won 155 and Bruguera 154. Sampras recorded about 60 unforced errors. In the past, he has had easier victories and better statistics, so what did he mean when he said that it was his best performance on clay?

Maybe Sampras himself doesn't have an explanation, but my answer is simple: The American had, at a very critical moment in the contest—at the beginning of the final set—entered the zone. He started playing beyond himself.

When the fifth set began, I noticed that Sampras's tongue was hanging out. To me, this is significant. It does so only if you are very relaxed, not mentally or physically tense. It's actually the natural position of the tongue, because in terms of human anatomy, it requires continuous muscular effort to keep the mouth closed and the tongue inside.

This little detail indicated that the normal control mechanisms of Sampras's mind and body had been bypassed. Moreover, the expression on his face was one of deep exhaustion and yet, paradoxically, he was playing his best tennis. In other words, he was tapping a layer of energy that transcended his usual reserves.

The fifth set began with Sampras winning his serve game to love. Then it was Bruguera's serve, and Sampras went all out to break it. This game—the most critical in the match—went over eight deuces, from one rally to the next, with an audience of 12,000 people screaming with excitement. It was the most fascinating and intense duel I've seen in a long time. In the end, Sampras broke Bruguera to make it 2–0.

The Spaniard was aware that he needed to gain a rebreak immediately, otherwise it would be very difficult for him to get back into the match. When Sampras's serve game is working, when he is consistently hitting the lines, it is difficult for his opponents to take even one point from him. But Bruguera managed to stretch this game over four deuces, gaining two break points. Sampras barely kept the edge and made it 3–0.

Both players were by now really exhausted, breathing heavily, sweating profusely, barely recovering at the changeover. My feeling is that Sampras, having just played three brilliant games in a zone space, now allowed his tactical mind to take over once more. Sitting on the bench, he must have been thinking, "My god, I'm up 3–0, but how am I going to physically survive the rest of this set?" So he changed his strategy, allowing Bruguera to win his serve games without putting up much of a fight, saving all his energy for his own serve game, hoping to win the match by holding on to the first crucial break.

At 5–3, Sampras was serving for the match and Bruguera, in an all-or-nothing effort, managed to win the first two points to reach 0–30. But Sampras was able to outplay him on the next four points, winning the game, the set, and a thrilling contest.

Sampras did not play a perfect match, but trying to play perfectly is not necessarily the same as being a brilliant and successful tennis player. That is why I begin the chapter with this anecdote. When a close-fought match goes into the fourth and fifth sets—which for professionals occurs only in the Grand Slams and Davis Cup—it often happens that the normal criteria of perfect tennis no longer apply.

In the best-of-three-sets contests of other tournaments, a professional like Sampras would never throw away as many points as he did in the fourth and fifth sets against Bruguera, but he was pushed so far beyond his limits that he had to gamble, take big risks, and break free of his usual mind-set.

PERFECTIONISM

In my years as a professional player and later as a coach, I have come across many, many people whose goal is to play perfect tennis, and this ambition has a crippling effect on their game. It does not allow them to experience those magical spaces when normal ways of thinking and playing are transcended, when the energy dynamic between the players takes them above and beyond everything they know about how to play the sport.

Perfection is highly valued in our culture as a working

ethic and in our general approach to life. It sounds like a worthy and legitimate ambition, but if you look deeper into the phenomenon, you can see the problems it creates. For example, if you have an idea about how to hit a perfect backhand, this is a concept that you have created in your mind as a result of coaching lessons or watching other players.

When playing a match, if you try to fulfill the ideal that you have created for yourself, you will pay a price. Your attention will be subtly divided. You are not totally present to the situation on the court, to what is happening right now between you and your opponent. You are trying to bridge the gap between an image in your mind and the reality of your performance. Moreover, if you fail to execute your ideal— and every stroke you make is going to be different—then you are likely to become very self-critical.

In tennis, perfectionism can develop into a true demon. I have seen countless players become utterly frustrated with themselves because they could not fulfill their own idealistic standards.

One of my students, a thirty-three-year-old university lecturer named George, was obsessed with the movement of his forehand. He was determined that the stroke should finish in a certain way, with the racket high over his shoulder.

As I watched him play one afternoon, he got into a spirited and close-fought contest with another player in which neither man was holding anything back. At set point, they entered a long and exciting rally, at the end of which George's opponent sent him a powerful cross-court ball that looked like a winning shot. But George managed to block it with his forehand and return the ball into his opponent's corner for the winning point.

I was about to congratulate George when he cursed

loudly and stopped in the middle of the court, repeating the forehand stroke several times, as if trying to improve on it.

"I'll never get that right," he complained.

"George," I said. "For heaven's sake, you just hit a great winner. What more do you want?"

He had won the set, but he could not relax and enjoy the feeling of success because his last shot was a hastily improvised blocking stroke in which his racket didn't follow through as he had wished.

Such reactions are not as rare as you might suppose. Any experienced coach will tell such a player that he did well, that he did exactly what was required. Maybe there was no other way to answer the ball than to just block it, maybe even Sampras or Agassi would have done the same in similar circumstances. Still, George was dissatisfied because he did not fulfill his ideal of the perfect stroke.

For these kinds of players, it takes a while to understand that playing good tennis, even great tennis, has nothing to do with fulfilling ideals, with making perfect textbook strokes. It has to do with your ability to respond intelligently to the challenge of the moment. This requires an open, flexible attitude from a mind that is not cluttered with preconceived notions.

A masterful player like Sampras doesn't put himself under the stress that he needs to perform each and every shot at an optimum level. As in the match with Bruguera, Sampras is able to raise his game in important moments—in tennis they call it the big points—and emerge victorious. That is why he was so happy. With the destructive attitude of the perfectionist, he would have sabotaged his own joy and sense of fulfillment.

In my experience, the attitude toward perfection is as

true about life in general as it is about tennis. If you judge yourself by predetermined ideals about how you should behave, then you will never allow yourself the luxury of feeling good about yourself and your achievements. Something will always be lacking in your quest for excellence and success.

SELF-CRITICISM

Self-criticism is a natural consequence of perfectionism, and it can be a tricky demon to understand because even great players like Steffi Graf seem to never be satisfied with themselves. When Graf leaves the court after a victory and faces the TV cameras, she often criticizes her game, saying that she is not completely happy with her form.

It's tempting to conclude that one reason why Graf is such an outstanding player is because of her self-criticism, that this attitude of never being satisfied helps to make her successful. As a consequence, parents may be tempted to turn Graf into some kind of role model for their children, saying, "Look at Steffi, she's never satisfied with herself, she keeps on striving. If you want to be as good as her, you should never be satisfied with yourself."

My sense of Graf is that she has incredible confidence in herself, in her strength, in her strokes, in her ability to remain centered in spite of injuries, personal problems, bad calls, or unforced errors. She is a great athlete with tremendous trust in her ability to run and retrieve. She loves the challenge of a close contest and is almost fearless when it comes to crunch points that make lesser players quake in the knees.

But in front of the public, Graf feels more comfortable criticizing herself than praising herself. After all, it's more polite and modest to talk about your weaknesses than your strengths. Also, in Graf's case, she is known to be superstitious, not wishing to tempt fate by appearing to boast. Her fear is that if she says, "Wow, I'm so happy! I played really, really well today!" then this euphoria will rebound in the next match.

In her case, the strategy works, but I would be cautious in making Graf's behavior a role model for upcoming young players. Her self-criticism is a smoke screen, a cover for a very powerful and resourceful player. She won three Grand Slam tournaments in 1995 and repeated this awesome achievement in 1996 with hardly any practice when injuries kept her preparation periods to a minimum.

Success is always relative. Because she did not play the Australian Open, Graf did not win the Grand Slam in '95 or '96 as she did in 1988 when she attained the highest possible achievement by winning the Golden Grand Slam—the four major tournaments plus the Olympic gold medal. But I have a suspicion that she must be more satisfied now than in '88, because she is conquering so many more obstacles in her personal life these days and still winning on the pro circuit.

For me, there is a difference between honestly evaluating my performance on the court and being self-critical. I want to acknowledge those areas where my game is lacking but in a loving way, not putting myself down nor cutting my energy nor adopting a negative attitude about myself.

Self-criticism usually contains an element of comparison, both with myself—how much better I have played on other occasions—and with others, and certainly such an attitude can produce impressive results in terms of social achievement. Quite often, it is the person who is driven by self-criticism, by a sense of envy or inferiority, who fights his way to the top of the social ladder, whether in sports, politics, business, or the entertainment industry.

But it is difficult for such people to ever reach a point where they can relax and enjoy life. Rather, they tend to become locked into a mind-set of continuous struggle in which a sense of personal fulfillment is forever postponed. There is always one more challenge to be overcome.

BOREDOM

The third demon is boredom, and with boredom I include frustration. The two tend to go hand in hand. For example, if a player feels stagnant, if he repeats the same mistakes over and over again, if he feels his game is going nowhere, not improving, this leads to a feeling of frustration, which is often not expressed directly.

If someone asks how his game is going, then rather than admit his frustration at not being able to improve, he is likely to say something like, "Oh, I'm bored with tennis. These days I'm spending more time on the golf course." But the problem doesn't go away, and the chances are high that after a short while on the golf course, this player will reach the same point of frustration. Then what? Sailing? Paragliding? Mountain biking?

It seems natural for players to get bored with any game if a certain stimulation is missing. People need new experiences to stay interested, curious, engaged, participating. But changing things on the outside, hopping from sport to sport, doesn't solve the basic problem.

To transform boredom is a beautiful challenge, because if you succeed you can apply the same lesson to any aspect of your life that may seem dull and repetitive. After all, isn't this also what many people do with their love relationships, moving from one partner to the next in order to keep stimulated?

When I was practicing tennis four hours every day as a professional, I would not acknowledge that I was bored. I'd just keep on going with the exercise drills, moving mechanically, hitting 400, 500, 600 balls, and as a result, I often ended up losing the quality, the sharpness of my game.

I was afraid that if I allowed myself to feel the boredom, I would stop practicing and then feel guilty because I would not be fulfilling my commitment to stay in shape. Also, I always practiced with a partner, so it was not just me. It was a codependent situation. If I decided to stop, who was my partner going to practice with? I would be letting him down.

Sometimes I would go on practicing against my natural inclination, just to fulfill my part of the bargain, just for the other person, hitting balls without really being present. Looking back, I can see that such decisions cost me my enjoyment of the game.

To me, boredom is a sign of intelligence. The more intelligent you are, the more quickly you get bored when life falls into a routine. After all, you are not a machine. It is not in your nature as a human being to do things mechanically and repetitively.

To recognize the feeling of boredom, to give yourself permission to feel it and acknowledge it—that it's okay to be bored—already creates a certain relief, a certain space inside, and the possibility of transforming this uncomfortable feeling into something different.

When I connect with the feeling of boredom and accept it—"This is the way I am feeling, and it's okay"—something new can occur. This is why I suggest that you face your boredom instead of trying to run over it.

There are a number of options people commonly explore when boredom strikes. They try out a new racket, switch partners, take lessons from a new coach. They cut down the number of hours they spend on the court. They experiment with different styles of play. These are all short-term solutions and may be all you need to reawaken your interest in the game.

For me, the real turning point came when I shifted my focus from the outside to the inside—from what was going on around the court to what was happening inside of me. This was the key through which I realized that my love affair with tennis could continue for years, because I could use it as a pathway to self-exploration and self-discovery.

For example, one powerful and easy way to shift your focus is to start observing your breathing. In a practice drill when you are hitting forehands down the line, just as you have done many times, shift your attention from the ball, from the stroke, to the way you are breathing. As you practice, notice how much air you take in, how much you give out, when exactly the pause comes between your breaths, and so on. Through this technique, you reenter the present moment, you find yourself in the here and now, where boredom cannot exist.

EXPECTATION

The fourth demon is expectation. Here, I would like to mention what happened to the German tennis player, Michael Stich. Stich, as I mentioned earlier, is a gifted player who, as soon as he reached the number two slot in the world rankings, had problems living up to the expectations created by this lofty position. In the Grand Slams he repeatedly failed to make it through the opening rounds.

Then, in October 1995, something happened to Stich that was apparently even worse than his poor performance on court. He severely injured a foot while playing an indoor tournament in Vienna and was out of action for half a year. During that time, he had to undergo two risky and intricate surgical operations.

Just ten weeks after the second operation, with virtually no match practice, he entered the '96 French Open. Nobody expected him to do well, and Stich himself declared that he was entering the tournament just to play a few games as a starting point on the road back to world-class competition.

Watching Stich in the opening rounds, I could see that his mood was light and carefree. There was no weight on his shoulders. He did not have to prove anything, either to himself or anyone else. He was just happy to be back on court with two good feet beneath him, rather like a bird that is allowed to fly again after many months in the cage.

In this carefree mood, Stich won the first round, then the second, then the third, and then suddenly everyone began to sit up and notice that something rather remarkable was happening to this man, whom some unkind media commentators had already written off as a has-been.

In the quarterfinals, Stich beat the formidable Thomas Muster, the "king of clay," the man who had won Paris the previous year. In the semifinal, he beat Mark Rosset from Switzerland, playing so well that afterward he joyfully declared, "This was the best match I've ever played."

Contrary to all expectations, including his own, Stich had reached the final. But there, everything changed. Facing the Russian player, Yevgeni Kafelnikov, Stich played good tennis but had lost that magical quality of carefree innocence that had carried him through the tournament—the quality of being happy in himself, for no special reason. It was a close match, but in the crucial moments, the Russian was better. Stich lost in straight sets.

What happened? For me, Stich's demise began when, after his semifinal victory over Rosset, he declared, "Now I want to win the tournament." That was the moment when he lost his innocence, his freedom from desire. Expectation had entered: the expectation to win.

Expectation is a demon that puts you into the future. You are more concerned with the end result than with what is happening now, here, in the present moment. Your energy has become divided. Now you are more businesslike, more calculating, more likely to follow a strategy of the mind than to rely on intuition and spontaneity.

In Stich's case, his downfall was only human. By the time he reached the final, he knew that he needed one more victory to make a footnote for himself in the annals of tennis history. With this triumph, so unexpected, so unpredictable, he would not only be a star but almost a legend—someone who would be talked about for years to come.

There was, however, one more match to be played, one more match to be won. Second place, although still a remarkable achievement, would not do. That's just the way things are in our competitive culture. Stich knew this, and it became a pressure on him, robbing him of his effortless ease, his lightness of being—and of victory.

His disappointment was revealed in his comments after the match. "With second place I can't buy anything," he complained. On a practical level, it was simply not true. Stich had just won several hundred thousand dollars. But on another, more subtle level, it was painfully accurate. He couldn't buy himself a place in the record books. He paid the price of falling victim to the demon of expectation.

IS THERE A WAY OUT?

While reading this chapter you may find yourself becoming hungry for tips or techniques that can easily and quickly help you escape from the grip of the four demons: perfectionism, self-criticism, boredom, and expectation.

For the player on the path, however, it is important to take time to notice these demons as they occur and to understand their nature. A man of Zen accepts the demons. This acceptance and understanding itself eases their grip. Transformation occurs through a combination of understanding, meditation, and the nurturing of affirmative attitudes that I describe in chapter 9.

Anyone Else?

A priest was walking alone in the mountains when he lost his way. It became dark and in a moment of carelessness he stumbled over a cliff. As the priest fell, he managed to grab hold of a small bush growing out of the rock wall. He clung desperately to the bush, suspended in total darkness, not knowing how far the ground lay beneath him. In his panic and fear, he raised his face to the heavens above him and appealed to the Lord God to save him.

"Is there anyone up there? Is there anyone up there?" he shouted to the sky.

"Yes, my son," boomed a mighty voice. "I am here."

"Ah, thank god! I am a priest, please save me!" cried the distraught man.

"Yes, my son, I will save you," said the voice. "Just trust in me, let go of the bush, and you will come to no harm."

The priest looked down into the blackness below him, thought for a moment and then, turning his face heavenward once more, cried out, "Is there anyone else up there?"

8
Fear:
The Killer
on the Court

Those eyes. They can give you the chills. Watching a slow-motion replay of Jana Novotna's facial expression as she runs to intercept the ball during an important match is one of the most intense things I have seen on television.

It has taken me a while to be able to watch her. When Novotna is playing in the later rounds of a big tournament, it has become a habit with me to watch the contest for only a few minutes and then find something else to do. Just recently, I realized why. It has nothing to do with her skill as a player. Novotna is one of the most gifted female players currently competing on the pro circuit. She deserves her ranking in the top ten.

It has something to do with her pain, her suffering, her fear. I don't know if Novotna herself is even aware of it, but the camera doesn't lie. When the pressure is on, when the stakes are high, her eyes are twice as big as normal. When she runs and dives for the ball, she looks as panic-stricken as someone who is trying to escape a bullet or trying to save a small child who is about to fall off a cliff. I see not only fear in her expression but also despair, as if she knows that, no matter how hard she tries, she isn't going to make it.

In spite of the despair, Novotna tries extremely hard. She really pushes herself, maybe harder than anybody else. But it seems to me that somewhere, hidden in her psyche, is the belief that it's never going to be enough.

Her talent usually gets her through the early rounds of a tournament, but when it really counts, when the crown of victory is only a few games away, she knows she is going to lose. Actually, *lose* is too weak an expression. To be more accurate, she knows that she will not survive.

This is why it is difficult for me to watch Novotna. It hurts to see an incredibly gifted player sabotaging herself again and again at the very moment when she could triumph. It hurts to see her nakedness exposed in the slow-motion replays, to see the panic in her eyes as she tries, match after match, to break through the barrier.

The media has found a way of labeling Novotna's problem. Among the top women professionals, she is the one who "doesn't have her nerves under control." She is acknowledged as a gifted athlete but dismissed as "emotionally unstable."

In the 1993 Wimbledon final, Novotna outplayed Steffi Graf and came very close to gaining the most prestigious title tennis can offer. She was leading Graf 4–1 in the final set and was ahead 40–15 in the sixth game. Up to this moment, she had been hitting effortless winners, as if playing in a dream world where nothing could go wrong. Then, within ten minutes, she lost everything in one of the most dramatic collapses in the history of the sport, and when the match was over, she wept bitter tears in the arms of the Duchess of Kent who was presenting the prizes.

In the '95 French Open, she was leading the American, Chanda Rubin, 5–0 in the final set and 40–0 in the sixth game—as big a lead as you can possibly hope to have. She lost 8–6. When Novotna falls, she falls hard, struck down by her own fear.

Fear of what? This is not an easy question to answer. I am no psychologist and I don't pretend that I can supply instant answers for complex problems. Still, there are a few observations that can be made—observations that, though related to Novotna, are relevant for many players at different levels of the game.

I notice with Novotna that she is always pushing herself, more so than any other female player, clenching her fists after making a point, pumping herself up, shouting "Come on, now!" in a very harsh way to herself. Her whole manner suggests that she is operating like an army commander in a war zone.

To me, her manner seems very masculine in these moments, and this may be significant, because when she is at her most brilliant, when she is really fulfilling her potential, she does not behave like that. Rather, she comes across as a strong but sensitive woman, someone who can make magic with the ball in a very artistic way, rather like a gifted musician who is able to conjure wonderful sounds from a violin.

In crucial matches, when she faces tough opposition—which is bound to happen in the later rounds of the big tournaments—the army commander takes over, and the artistic genius seems to be crushed. But the price she pays for this overriding male energy is clear: Her gifts desert her.

TRUSTING FEMININE QUALITIES

I suspect that it is difficult for Novotna to trust her feminine qualities as a player, and this attitude must have developed during her younger years, as an adolescent, while she was being trained. It is no secret that in the rough, tough world of professional tennis trainers—the vast majority of whom are men—there are many coaches who are not respectful toward female players.

Women are often treated as inadequate versions of the male tennis player, as men in female bodies—who, try as they might, can never run as fast or hit as hard as the opposite sex. Moreover, when male coaches get together on social occasions and the beer has been flowing for a while, you tend to hear macho remarks passed about their female players including denigrating comments about their weight, looks, and sex appeal.

My guess is that Novotna received the message early in her career that she should not trust her talents as a woman—her sensitivity, her genius, her artistry—but should instead adopt a military style of discipline in order to become as physically strong as possible plus an attitude of pushing herself to her limits, never relaxing for a moment into the pleasure of the game, never thinking that, just the way she is, she is good enough.

Novotna's difficulty is reflected in the lives of many female tennis players. There seems to be a split between their essentially feminine nature and the demand that they should perform like men, being told that success lies in hitting harder and dominating their opponents through raw muscle power. The fear is that, because they are women, they will never make the grade and will be criticized for their inadequacies by whatever male authority figure is ruling their lives: the coach, the father, the teacher.

I am not suggesting that female players should be devoid of qualities like physical power and strength. In the demanding world of Grand Slam tournaments, a woman needs to be at the peak of her athletic potential, with plenty of punch in her serves and strokes.

What seems important, however, is that there should be no internal conflict. In Carl Gustav Jung's view of the human psyche, each individual—whether man or woman—possesses both masculine and feminine polarities. If one polarity is too heavily suppressed or rejected, then there is bound to be internal disharmony. Both sides need to be honored and respected.

EVERT AND HINGIS

Several female players have demonstrated that this inner harmony is possible. Chris Evert, the American champion who dominated women's tennis for several years in the 1970s, was able to combine power and strength with female grace and artistry. Steffi Graf, the most athletic and powerful female player currently in the game, also seems relaxed in her femininity and has blossomed from an awkward teenager into a beautiful woman.

Martina Hingis, the talented fifteen-year-old from Switzerland who beat Arancha Sanchez Vicario and Novotna to reach the semifinals of the '96 U.S. Open, seems to be developing in the graceful manner of a modern-day Chris

Evert. At her age, she lacks the muscle power of an adult and is proof of how far you can succeed in the game with an effortless swinging stroke. Interestingly, Hingis has been trained mostly by her mother, not by a male coach.

In many ways, Hingis will be a player to watch in coming years, to see how her style develops and whether she can become the undisputed number one player, winning through skilfull use of her female power.

TOTAL EXPOSURE

It may seem to be an unnecessary intrusion into the lives of professional tennis players to attempt to look beneath the surface of their behavior, as I have done with Novotna. But with a sport like tennis, this examination is hard to avoid, because when professional players, male or female, are on the court, everything is on display for public view. Put yourself in their place for a moment and you will see why this is true. Imagine you are on center court.

- ° You are alone.
- ° There are no teammates to support you.
- ° You cannot speak to your coach.
- ° There are no time-outs in which to discuss strategy.
- ° There are 15,000 people watching your every move and millions more watching on television.
- ° You are competing against the finest players in the game.
- ° You oh-so-badly want to win.
- ° And after every point, in the pause between serves, the

TV stations will rerun your movements in slow motion, showing every nuance of expression on your face.

In this kind of situation, you are probably going to feel like an overripe tomato in a pressure cooker with the gas turned up high. It is a situation in which any kind of personal weakness, any old psychological wounds, any unresolved issues—maybe dating back to your childhood—are likely to be exposed.

This, to me, is what makes professional tennis so fascinating. It's not just the score—who wins, who loses—it's the human drama of whether an individual can meet and overcome the major challenges that he or she is bound to face in such critical situations. Under such circumstances, even the best professionals suffer from fear of failure, especially when they are representing not just themselves but their country, such as in the Davis Cup and Federation Cup.

DAVIS CUP PRESSURES

I was talking about Michael Stich in the previous chapter and I mention him again here because of an incident that happened in 1995, shortly before he injured his foot. Stich was playing a crucial singles match for Germany in the Davis Cup semifinal against Russia. The stakes were high. If Stich won, Germany would go into the final against the United States. If he lost, his country also lost.

At the end of the fifth set, Stich had used up a total of eight match points, enough for any player to normally make a winning shot and deliver the anticipated victory. It didn't happen. I watched—the whole of Germany watched—as Stich's skill, confidence, and energy slowly evaporated from the TV screen, eaten up by a steadily increasing fear of not being able to make it.

His defeat did not happen all at once. Whenever he was behind, his energy would seem to reignite, and he would fight his way back. But each time victory came within his grasp, just a point away, he was unable to do it. Eventually, the inevitable happened and Stich walked off the court feeling as bad as it is possible for a tennis player to feel.

For Stich, the experience was a catastrophe because he tried so hard, he put so much effort into gaining those eight precious match points, only to throw them away with strokes that ought to be reserved for beginners. But he is not alone; many talented players from many different countries have succumbed to the pressure of the Davis Cup and been unable to play their best tennis.

These people fail because they try too hard, and they try too hard because under these conditions it's not just a matter of personal victory. It's an issue of national pride, national honor, and this responsibility weighs so heavily on them that they end up completely stiff in their bodies, as if half-paralyzed.

As a Zennis player, you need to be at ease with the possibility of losing, not just as an individual but also as a representative of whatever school, club, team, or country has chosen you. Only then can you be relaxed enough to focus on your game and play according to your potential. If you are too concerned with your responsibility, then you will also become too concerned with the outcome of the match. As a result, you are bound to miss the many important steps that might otherwise have led you to victory.

SHARING YOUR FEARS

Looking at fear from another perspective, I would like to relate an incident that occurred a couple of years ago when I was giving coaching lessons to Harold, a seventy-five-year-old retired businessman who had only recently decided to take up tennis.

For a beginner, he was doing pretty well. After a couple of lessons, I asked him a very simple question: "What is happening?"

Harold hesitated, as if wondering whether to say what was on his mind, then confessed, "I'm just amazed how much fear I have."

"Fear of what?" I queried.

"Fear of missing the ball," he replied.

Actually, Harold was making most of his shots. He wasn't missing so many—not enough to justify such a strong reaction. So I stopped the lesson and suggested to Harold that he should adopt a friendly attitude toward his fear and, instead of trying to push it away, listen to any message that might be hidden in it.

We sat together in a quiet corner of the court, and I asked Harold to close his eyes and see if he could remember any similar feelings from his past. It didn't take long. Soon Harold started to tell me about his experience of playing baseball at school and how embarrassed he was when he struck out or failed to make a clean catch.

"I can still recall the screams of derision around me and the insults when I made a mistake," he said.

When I encouraged him to give these old feelings permission to surface, tears were soon running down his cheeks. He sobbed heavily as he recalled specific incidents when he had been taunted and ridiculed.

To me, it was a real insight to see how a man can keep a traumatic memory, an emotional imprint, in the unconscious part of his mind for more than sixty years, unhealed and un-resolved, so that when he picks up an innocent-looking object like a tennis racket, he starts to feel fear.

After sharing this with me, Harold wondered whether he ought to stop playing tennis because of these painful memories, but I strongly encouraged him to keep playing. I was sure that the healing process would happen for him most effectively by staying in the situation that had provoked the memory.

We carried on playing tennis together for the next few weeks and, as I suspected, Harold's ability to have fun and enjoy himself on the court increased tremendously. Having exposed and understood his wound, he gradually lost his fear of missing the ball and suddenly one day broke out into spontaneous laughter on the court. He was free from his ghosts, free to be himself.

THE MANY FACES OF FEAR

In the examples that I have given, Novotna, Stich, and Harold all suffered from fear:

° Novotna's fear of not being good enough, and being stigmatized as the biggest underachiever in women's world class tennis.

° Stich's desire to be acclaimed the national hero and his consequent fear of letting his country down.

° Harold's fear of missing the ball and being ridiculed.

Whatever the fear, the method of dealing with it remains the same. There is no need to suppress it or push it away. That will only give it more energy and strength. Make friends with your fear, listen to it, receive it as a message from your own psyche. There is bound to be some wisdom, some hidden treasure locked inside this apparently unwelcome sensation. With wisdom there always comes, as a natural by-product, a feeling of liberation.

In concluding this chapter, I will mention a few more fears commonly encountered by tennis players at different levels of the game:

- Fear of losing your image as a winner when trailing in a match with a lesser-ranked player.

- Fear of showing your nasty sides, of losing your image as a nice, polite player whom everyone likes.

- For beginners, especially, fear of looking stupid in comparison to more experienced players.

- Fear of not being physically attractive or athletic enough. Any little comment made in this direction can be very discouraging.

- For people who play in teams, fear of not making the actual playing squad when there are more players available than slots. It's the fear of being excluded.

- Fear of being too good. This sounds odd, but is quite common among talented young players who realize that if they want to fulfill their potential, they must leave the security of the hometown environment, their friends, their local club, and head off into unknown territory. Basically, it's the fear of being lonely at the top.

THE BASIC FEAR

All these fears can be reduced to the fear of being alone. If we are willing and able to rely on ourselves, to stand on our own feet, then any fear of being criticized or rejected by others would automatically lose its grip.

This basic fear of being alone comes from childhood. It is the experience we all had as little children when, in order to survive, we needed other people to take care of us. As adults, we are capable of looking after ourselves, but if the child's fear continues to dominate us from within, it's difficult to trust that we can really be okay.

For the Zennis player, exploring fear can be a fascinating journey. It may begin at the point where fear is a killer, but it can end in the recognition that fear is your friend, a signpost for self-discovery, an opportunity for greater self-understanding and maturity.

As a player on the path you are bound to come face-to-face with all of the apparently negative qualities that I have described in the last two chapters. Now it's time to introduce the four jewels—attitudes that can help you overcome and transform these formidable obstacles.

That's All?

A samurai came home unexpectedly one day and found his servant making love with his wife. He pulled the man outside and said, "I am going to kill you, but I am an honorable man and I will give you a chance. Take my second sword and defend yourself."

The servant, who had no experience in sword fighting, begged the samurai to give him time to say farewell to his spiritual master, a Zen mystic. "Since my death is certain, please allow me to pay my final respects to this holy man," he pleaded.

"Very well," said the samurai, "you have one hour."

Running to the mystic, the servant fell on his knees, weeping, and cried, "My life is finished!" He explained the situation and asked for any guidance that might help him to survive the coming duel.

"Be total," said the mystic.

"That's all?" queried the bewildered servant.

"That is enough," said the mystic and turned away.

The servant returned home, picked up the sword, and hurled himself at the samurai, striking out blindly with all his strength.

The samurai was shocked by the unorthodox manner with which the servant was fighting. He was accustomed to the ritual and finesse of fighting other samurais. He had no answer to the furious onslaught of this unskilled amateur.

"Stop! You deserve to live," said the samurai and, sheathing his sword, gave the servant his freedom.

9
The Four Jewels:
Being with What Is, Staying in the Middle, Totality, and Playfulness

A bad call on a crucial point. It happens to every player, sooner or later, especially to those who play tournaments. In this particular instance, it happened to a world class female player, Anke Huber, who was playing the promising young Slovak, Karina Habsudova, in the fourth round of the 1996 French Open.

Huber had dominated the first set and had arrived at set point, when the ace that would have given her the set was called out. Immediately she walked to the net and pointed to the spot where the ball had bounced, indicating that she wanted the umpire to come down from his seat and inspect the mark on the clay. The umpire did so, and confirmed the out call.

Huber was visibly upset and wanted to protest. The umpire, an Italian man with a rather patronizing manner, smiled and shrugged his shoulders as if to say, "Well, you silly woman, what do you want me to do? Out is out."

Huber threw her racket on the ground in a childish, petulant manner, like a six-year-old scolded by an authoritarian parent whom she was powerless to disobey. She had to pick up the racket and continue playing, but her composure had completely disappeared, and she lost the match in straight sets.

In fact, the call was bad. Those watching the slow-motion replay on television could clearly see Huber's ball hit the line. So a bad call cost her the set and probably the match, plus the chance to continue to the next round of a Grand Slam tournament. It shouldn't really happen, but it does. In tennis, as in life, bad calls do happen—like it or not—and they can be expensive, especially if they cause a player to collapse emotionally or psychologically.

This anecdote leads me to the first of four jewels that I am going to talk about in this chapter. By *jewels* I mean qualities that can help players give their best performance, attitudes that encourage more awareness and consciousness.

BEING WITH WHAT IS

The essence of this quality is that if you can fully accept and allow any feeling or emotion that has arisen in you, with no holding back—in other words, if you can be with it—it will release itself and disappear. If you resist the feeling, it will persist, it will disturb you, and it will continue to affect your behavior.

As a personal coach, both in tennis and in business management, I know that if an individual shares something intimate with me, something that has been hidden, something that this person fears or judges as bad or wrong, then the negative emotional charge around the issue immediately begins to dissipate.

An alchemy happens in sharing that brings about a powerful transformation, and this alchemy has to do with acceptance. Once the person feels that I am listening attentively, not judging, not condemning, just accepting him as he is, a parallel feeling of self-acceptance starts to arise in him. It is this self-acceptance that produces the magic, that does the job, that transforms the negative energy.

In a singles match on a tennis court there is no opportunity to share an unwanted feeling with anyone, but the alchemy of self-acceptance remains the same. Once a player has had the experience of being accepted in his totality by someone else, he can apply the alchemy of self-acceptance when he is standing alone at the baseline. He knows the secret. He can be with what is. A second party is not required.

Let us see how this understanding might have operated in the case of Anke Huber. First of all, it was immediately apparent that the bad call affected her strongly. She badly wanted to win the match against Habsudova, who can be one of the toughest opponents for any female player, and in Huber's mind, she had already won the first set with her ace. But no, the point was disallowed, and instead of having the set tucked safely under her belt, she had to win it all over again.

Watching the incident, I noticed that she was unable to deal with her feeling of frustration at being cheated. She must also have felt put down by the umpire, who, as I already mentioned, dealt with the incident in a rather patronizing manner.

In terms of being with what is, Huber would at that

moment have needed to get in touch with her emotional truth, to allow it and give it a form of expression and release. My hunch was that her emotional truth was basically anger.

True, she tried to express herself. She threw her racket down, but it was a half-hearted gesture of protest, done in a rather wimpish way. She was already fighting against the feeling within herself, knowing that if she really let loose and threw the racket at the umpire, which I suspect is what she really wanted to do, she would be fined or even disqualified. So she played safe, acting like a sulky, rebellious child who wants to show her discontent even though a large, powerful father figure is standing over her and saying, "Don't you dare!"

In suppressing her anger, Huber throttled her own energy. She continued to play, but the internal conflict sabotaged her drive and her composure, which against a tough opponent like Habsudova was enough to ensure her defeat.

What Huber could have done, as a crucial first step, was to take a few seconds to fully accept the fact that she was angry, to really allow this feeling inside herself, to say yes to it, without trying to condemn or deny it. This, in itself, would have been enough to keep her fully present, in the here and now, connected with her own energy, not lost in reaction and internal conflict.

Then, once she had owned the feeling, she could have explored a number of avenues of expression. For example, she could have stamped her feet—not like a child but like a warrior—which in my experience is an easy and effective method of expressing anger and a way to stay centered and grounded while you do so. At the same time, she could have shouted loudly, "No! No! No!" not at the umpire, but turning her back on him and directing it up into the sky.

In other words, she could have made an authentic show of strength and power, which would have allowed her to maintain a certain integrity, as if to say, "The jerk in the fancy suit might be able to deny me the point, but he cannot crush my energy. I trust my gut feeling that it's a bad call and I am right to challenge it."

There are other alternatives. She could have made a show of refusing to accept the umpire's decision by standing her ground, glaring silently at him over the net, releasing her anger through her eyes, making him feel uncomfortable and hesitant about returning to his chair.

She could have expressed her anger by arguing with him. Some players are experts at this. For example, Martina Navratilova would have questioned the umpire in a staccato of words for five minutes. She might not have succeeded in altering his decision, but she would have released her frustration, made her presence felt, and stayed connected with her energy while having the satisfaction of giving the umpire a hard time. Billie Jean King was also good at this and so, of course, were Connors and McEnroe.

My only caution to players who feel inclined to argue with umpires is that it should be done selectively and with care, so that you do not find yourself out of the tournament. Rules of conduct have been tightened in recent years, partly in response to the behavior of Connors and McEnroe. Andre Agassi was disqualified from the 1996 Indianapolis tournament for swearing at an umpire.

You may not have thought about it, but the referee is an archetypal authority figure and as such is likely to evoke whatever conflicts you have with authority. How you react depends on how you learned to deal with authority as a child. You may find yourself sulking, fighting, shouting, seducing, feeling helpless, collapsing, being tricky, or rationalizing your reactions.

As a Zennis player, this situation offers you an opportunity to see how you respond to authority and to find creative ways to keep yourself vitally alive and centered. For example, walking back to the baseline, Anke Huber could have shouted, "There is no god! There is no justice!"

Theatrical? Yes, but these amateur dramatics would help her to release emotional energy rather than being devoured by it. My feeling is that if Huber had allowed herself to be a bit more of an actress, she would have found it a lot easier to stay energized on the court.

One difficulty in mastering the art of being with what is is that many players find themselves in a state of energetic collapse before they realize what has happened. They are overwhelmed by their reactions and by the time they pause to assess the situation, they have already moved into a sense of hopelessness, defeat, and collapse. It can go very fast.

But even at this stage it is not too late. This is also an opportunity to recognize what is happening, to accept it, and practice the jewel of being with what is.

As before, the first and most important step is to catch yourself here, now, in this new state, to acknowledge that "Right now, I am collapsed." This may sound easy, but it is rare to come across a player who can do this for the simple reason that the state of collapse is one that players dread. The belief is that "If I collapse, I am finished." So the tendency is to fight against the feeling with a kind of grim determination usually reserved for sea captains who decide to go down with a sinking ship.

The main reason why such states persist is because players become paralyzed, entering into a kind of numb denial of what is happening to them, or they pretend that nothing has happened and try to maintain a winning attitude. In both cases they are fighting against their own energetic reality.

To understand that "Yes, I am collapsed" is to stay in tune with your energy. This staying in tune allows the possibility of change, because a fundamental law of energy is that it needs to move. Movement is intrinsic to its nature. So when you stay in tune with your energy you are going to move with it, sooner or later, to a new state. It is only when you resist your energy that it becomes stuck or blocked.

The key here is to accept the situation and breathe deeply into your belly. You are collapsed, but you don't have to go dead; it's too early to enter your grave. Deep breathing into your belly helps you stay vitally alive. You can do this between points and during the changeover after every second game.

Once you realize and accept that you are in a collapsed state, you can relax. The worst has happened and maybe it even feels like the match is lost. But now you can start from scratch. Even if you are deep into the third set and trailing badly on points, you can adopt the attitude of beginning the match anew. Things didn't turn out the way you hoped, but there is no need to blame yourself. With a curious attitude, you can see what will happen instead of the great victory you planned. Just keep breathing into your belly, staying open to the new, the unexpected, the unknown.

It may be that you will still lose, but the nature of a tennis match is such that it gives you many, many chances to reenter the contest. It's never over until match point has been reached and passed.

You can come back after having collapsed. And if you do not, then by accepting your collapse you will spare yourself the torture that many players put themselves through when they walk off the court, beating themselves up for having lost a match that, according to the rankings or their own expectations, they should have won.

Having consciously experienced and accepted the state of collapse a few times, you will find that it has lost its grip over you. The fear of this state, the feelings of shame and embarrassment associated with it, become less and less of an issue.

STAYING IN THE MIDDLE

This jewel refers to a tendency among many players, especially those who have not acquired much experience in tournaments, to become overly concerned with winning and losing.

For example, it sometimes happens that new players on the pro circuit hit a flow of success for a certain period, with most of the matches going their way. Then, once they have reached a high position in the rankings, they tend to lose the flow. Why? Because their attitude changes. They start trying to defend the position they have attained, and that is a sure killer to good form on the court.

The attitude of seasoned professionals is that you can't afford to be concerned about your ranking. In the manner of Zen, they know that the only thing you can do is take one match at a time. The only security you've got is to play the next match as well as you can, coming fresh to the game.

The real masters develop an attitude that is almost like nonchalance. From them, you hardly ever hear bravado statements like "I'm going to beat that guy" or "I am the best." These players are masters because they know how easily they can lose a match against an opponent who is having a good day and because they are able to accept the loss without putting themselves down.

They have gone through the heaven and hell of winning and losing many times, and they have learned the knack to stay in the middle, not bragging when they win, not getting depressed when they lose.

There is a great temptation, when you win an important match, to take yourself too seriously, especially if you happen to beat one of the tournament favorites. And the media is likely to amplify this temptation by immediately proclaiming you the next great hope for your city or your country.

Then the going gets tough because, as your winning streak continues, you start to attract more and more attention from the top players. You become the man to beat.

This happened a few years back to a young German player called Marc Kevin Goellner, who out of nowhere shot up to number thirty in the world rankings, beating stars like Ivan Lendl, Stefan Edberg, and Michael Chang. He had an incredible six-month run, helping to win the Davis Cup for his country and earning the title Baby Boom Boom from the media as the heralded successor to Boom Boom Becker. But then he crashed.

One reason why Goellner could not continue his run was that other top players started to study his game, probing for weaknesses, exploring ways to beat him. Once one player had found the way, the others successfully copied the strategy. In addition, Goellner was not able to handle the sudden fame, the million-dollar contracts, the expectations that he was heading rapidly for the world's top ten. As a result, he quickly sank to number 150 before recovering and settling down at around number 80.

Another pitfall is when players overreact to losses, walking off the court thinking, "Oh my god, I should never have lost that one. I am so bad. I am a failure." The danger here is that you start to create a negative self-image that will make things more difficult in your next tournament. As you walk out onto the court, there may be demons in your head whispering, "It's going to be just like last time. I'm not going to make it."

A champion like Pete Sampras does not blame himself after a defeat. He simply says, "Well, so-and-so played really well today and he deserved to win," almost with the detachment of a Zen monk who declares, "When I'm hungry, I eat, when I'm tired, I sleep."

Such bland statements don't provide much food to a story-hungry media and for many years Sampras had the image of being a rather boring guy, but he continued to be so successful that eventually his critics had to change their tune. In my view, an important key to Sampras's success lies in his blasé attitude, because he remains in the middle, unperturbed by victory or defeat.

So remember, when you win, don't try to make it the main topic of conversation for the next six weeks in your local club. When you lose, don't make that a big story, either. Stay in the middle.

TOTALITY

I would like to introduce the third jewel by mentioning George Gurdjieff, one of this century's best-known and most provocative mystics. Gurdjieff used to tell his disciples that there are four layers of human energy, and that usually nobody penetrates beyond the first layer.

He devised all kinds of exhausting and arduous practices to give his disciples an experience of the second layer—such as digging a ditch for hours and then filling it in again—and several of those who followed his instructions reported extraordinary experiences of suddenly being filled with tremendous energy when a moment earlier they were feeling utterly exhausted.

Such experiences are the product of totality, of throwing yourself into an activity with your total effort for a long period. One of the by-products of totality in a sport like tennis is that it becomes much easier to play well when you have gone beyond the normal, daily, first layer of human energy.

Professional players sometimes play four or five hours a day during practice periods because they know that a lot can happen in the last two hours, after they have been hitting hundreds of balls. This is because the mind gets tired, the body gets tired, and suddenly a new layer of energy gets tapped and provides a second wind.

When you play like this, your mind is going to object many times, saying things like, "Oh my god, I can't go on anymore." But if you are a reasonably healthy person, you can take the risk of pushing the envelope a little further, trusting that you have more reserves of energy waiting to be tapped.

If you don't listen to your mind and keep on playing, there is a good chance that you will enter the Zen space, where the game is playing you, where the mind is silent and the body knows exactly what to do, where strokes and moves that seemed awkward before now seem easy and effortless.

Quite recently, I had an unexpected experience of this state when, late one evening—around ten o'clock—I started to play table tennis with Steve, a friend of mine who is a Ping-Pong enthusiast and has a table in his second garage.

I hadn't touched a table tennis paddle in ten years, and I thought we'd maybe play best of three sets and then call it a night. I didn't manage to win more than nine points in the first two sets. Steve's spins were so tricky that even with my considerable experience in ball games, I was unable to read the way he was cutting the ball and returning it back over the net.

"Come on, let's play another round," said Steve.

"Okay," I said, curious to see how my responses would develop.

We kept on playing, set after set, and for some reason it became irrelevant that it was one o'clock in the morning and the night was passing. After three hours of playing very rusty table tennis, but with absolute totality, something started to click in my game. I began to return Steve's spins with consistency. My backhand, which had not worked all evening, now started to be a winning stroke. I started to take more risks, hitting spin shots with more courage and authority and watching the ball do what I wanted. As if in trance, I won my first set.

The table tennis got better and better—not just mine but Steve's as well. We fell into a hypnotic state that was ruled by the clack-clack, clack-clack of the Ping-Pong ball and the rhythmic sound of our breathing. By the time we finally stopped, somewhere around three in the morning, after playing a total of five hours, I had won almost half the sets.

In the space of totality, my game had improved significantly, whereas in the usual course of events, we would have stopped after an hour or so, with me doubting if I should ever return to the Ping-Pong table.

Returning to the full-sized courts, it can be asked, How can you play your heart out in a game like tennis where you have so many breaks, so much stopping and starting? The question is relevant because it is in the nature of tennis that you rarely exhaust yourself physically during a match, especially if you are not among the top professionals who play five-set matches in the Grand Slams.

With club and social players, an average match lasts sixty minutes, and within this period you spend a great deal of time picking up balls, changing sides, and preparing to play. The average rally lasts no more than four strokes, then you stop, walk back to the baseline, and get ready to play the next point.

In this way, tennis is very different from, say, long distance running, in which you are moving continuously for sixty minutes. As a runner, whether you like it or not, you are going to exhaust yourself. Totality is built into the design of long-distance running. Not so in tennis.

With this understanding, it is helpful to develop a practice routine that gives you a real chance to play your heart out. You can do this by agreeing with a friend or group of friends to meet once every two or three weeks and play a tennis marathon: two hours in the morning and two in the afternoon, not stopping even when you become tired.

The experience of totality in practice will give you much more confidence to play with your full energy during competition. You may have noticed that your mind tends to be miserly in calculating what you can afford to do with your energy. It is always warning you not to risk too much, not to exhaust yourself, not to waste precious reserves of strength. You have to save it for later, hold it back, measure it out.

But now you know that there is much more energy available than you thought possible. You can give your all, allowing your energy to be expressed with totality in each stroke, each rally, trusting that when the point of exhaustion is reached, fresh energy will be tapped. You will soon discover that your trust is rewarded by a higher standard of play.

PLAYFULNESS

In chapter 7, I was talking about Michael Stich and his impressive performance at the 1996 French Open when he reached the singles final just ten weeks after a major operation on his foot.

For me, the best match of the tournament, and one of the most significant that took place during that whole year, was the quarterfinal in which Stich beat Thomas Muster, who at that time was the undisputed "king of clay," a man who had become so good at winning on clay courts that most of the world's top players seemed to be avoiding the tournaments in which he was competing.

Muster's tactic is to rely on his awesome stamina and his ability to keep the ball in play. He is not a serve-and-volley specialist. He doesn't often come to the net. He rarely goes for risky shots. He just runs and runs and runs, returning every shot, every ball, and the slower clay surfaces allow him to reach and return balls that on faster surfaces would be just impossible. Eventually, out of frustration, exhaustion, or overeagerness, his opponents start making errors and Muster picks up the points.

Nobody expected Stich, the delicate artist, to beat Muster, the marathon man. The general opinion among experts and amateurs alike was that Stich had no chance, and when the contest began, it looked as though this opinion would prove correct.

Muster won the first set 6–4 and broke Stich early in the second set for a 3–2 lead. True to form, Muster was answering everything his opponent could offer and making Stich run around so badly that he already seemed exhausted. At the changeovers, Stich could be seen sitting panting on the bench, his chest heaving as he tried to recover from the effort of keeping up with Muster.

Somehow Stich managed a rebreak to make it 3–3, and then a big change occurred. He became so calm, so composed, not panting, not gasping for air. Clearly, Stich had tapped into a new layer of energy. It was also obvious to me that he had entered the zone.

He began playing such aesthetic, beautiful, relaxed tennis that it was a joy to watch him. While everybody else in the tournament seemed determined to use every ounce of power and muscle to produce hard balls, Stich belonged to a different species. Even with his fast shots he seemed to only caress the ball, so that it left his racket effortlessly but with dazzling accuracy.

You could see that Stich had become happy with himself, in love with his creativity on the court. He was in such intimate rapport with the ball that it seemed to land exactly where he wanted. He could mix 200 kmh serves with subtle, drop-dead shots that would fall just over the net like ripe tomatoes. Even when he hit a blistering serve it never looked like hard work, and I was left wondering where his power was coming from.

What was even more remarkable: Stich was beating Muster at his own game, winning rallies from the baseline and putting the clay expert under the kind of pressure that is normally reserved for his opponents. In the fourth set, when Stich came back from 2–5 to win the tie break 7–6, it was Muster's turn to get nervous and start missing balls.

Moreover, when Stich was trailing 2–5 in this crucial set, he made no special effort. He kept on playing almost casually, not trying to attack more, not pushing himself, and then suddenly, seemingly by pure luck, the score was 5–5.

Observing this, one TV commentator said that Stich could have beaten Muster more easily if he had been more aggressive, running to the net more often. This simply reveals the commentator's misunderstanding of what was happening. If Stich had followed a preplanned strategy of coming to the net, he would have been more predictable, and Muster would have had all the answers.

Stich did come to the net, but not consistently, not predictably. To find the thread of how to move rightly in such a match—as Stich did—is a masterpiece of intuition and spontaneity.

The thing that made this match so distinctive and unusual is that Stich really enjoyed himself. He was like a dancer reveling in his dance, delighting in each graceful step or movement. This, to me, is the essence of a playful attitude, an example of how tennis can be played when the deadly seriousness of competition has lost its grip on a player.

I do not mean to suggest that during this three-hour match Stich had no moments of worry or concern. Many times he may have been thinking things like, "Wow, I can really beat this guy! I can make it to the semifinal!"

In a match of this length and importance, the mind is bound to come up with all kinds of ambitions and fears, but Stich's overall mood of playfulness, his lack of concern about the outcome, his gratitude at being able to come this far in his first Grand Slam since his operation, carried him beyond the grip of his own seriousness. He won the match in Zen style.

Playfulness is a difficult quality to define. Sometimes, you may have experienced being playful on the court but at the cost of losing a match. In other words, you were goofing around and got careless.

When I talk about playfulness, I don't mean that you lose concentration and alertness. I don't mean that you hit the ball carelessly. I don't mean that you start slacking off. I mean that you are no longer gripped by the seriousness of competition, by the compelling need to win, by an attitude of grim effort and struggle.

Paradoxically, once you are free of the compulsion to win, your chances of winning are likely to increase. As Jerry May, Monica Seles's therapist, has observed, "One of the psychological factors of success is that people can enjoy themselves and have fun."

On the tennis court, having fun translates as an attitude of spontaneity, of moment-to-moment creating. There is no planning, no mental activity. It's a flow, a dance, a play of energy. You are not hindering the flow. You just step out of the way and let it happen. In this state there is trust in yourself, there is happiness, and there is also a certain gratitude about being alive and experiencing this delightful moment.

JEWELS VS. DEMONS

As players on the path, we have a choice: to practice the four jewels or to fall victim to the four demons and the killer on the court. When you play, especially in practice sessions, you can make a conscious choice to be playful rather than serious, to play with totality rather than trying to be perfect, to be with what is, rather than indulging in self-criticism.

There is no shortcut, however. The demons are going to come up, especially during match play. The real solution lies in a fundamental change of attitude toward your game as a whole, and that transformation I call Zen.

A Fine Archer

A local official was visiting a school for Zen archery. Watching one student shoot several arrows into the exact center of a target, he commented to the master, "My, my! This fellow is an excellent archer!"

"It may seem so to you," said the master, "and it is true that on his own he does quite well. But when he competes for a brass farthing with other archers, his knees begin to shake, and when he shoots for a bag of silver, his hands tremble so badly that he can hardly hold the bow."

10
Zennis on the Court

If you learn the principles of Zennis, you will soon be able to play meditatively in practice situations with a coach or a friend. You will feel that you have mastered the art of being in the moment, breathing freely, acting spontaneously, and playing clean, unworried shots. You will be unconcerned about the outcome of the game and may even enjoy hitting a ball out of play if the stroke gives you a nice feeling.

But a word of caution: There is a lot of difference between practice games and a real match. The fire test for the Zennis player is in a situation where, for some obvious or more subtle reason, it suddenly matters who wins. Then things tend to change quite dramatically.

For example, you may find yourself playing against a friend who has beaten you five times in a row. Up to now, it's been okay—a learning situation for you. But here you are again, one set down, two games behind in the second, and this time you want to change the pattern. You don't want to be beaten. This time, you want to win.

For me, and for many tennis players, the pressure to win, to do well, is felt most acutely in team tennis, when playing for a club, a school, a state, even for a country—in other words, in any team situation from the local junior high school all the way to the Davis Cup.

When you are playing just for yourself and the result doesn't turn out right, you can maybe shrug it off, thinking, "Well, better luck next time." But with your teammates around, and with each match contributing to the overall score between Team A and Team B, you don't want to be the one who lets the side down.

This is an interesting phenomenon, because when you play a singles match—even in a team contest—you need to play for yourself. You need to be entirely focused on your own game, not thinking about your fellow team members and the overall situation. But, like it or not, the added pressure is there, weighing on you, and everybody who has played in team competition knows what I'm talking about.

I'm not saying this pressure is necessarily a stress factor, because it affects people differently. Some players thrive on it, and others become so nervous—so worried about letting their side down and being condemned by their teammates—that they are hardly able to hold the racket straight, let alone get their first serve in.

I've noticed over the years that I'm one of those players who does better in a team, when a match means more than just a personal win. I tend to hang in longer and fight harder than I would otherwise.

Over the years, in team tennis, I must have played more

than a dozen matches that went to a tie breaker in the final set, and I won all of them, while in open tournaments—playing just for myself as an individual—I have hardly ever played a tie break in the final set. Why? Because I just wouldn't fight that long.

The main point to grasp here is that Zennis may seem easy when you're in a practice situation, but when you're under pressure, when for some reason you really want to win—your girlfriend or boyfriend is watching, your parents are in the crowd, the team is depending on you—then it's a different story. Then you have to deal with all kinds of things inside yourself that were not visible before.

THE SAME MISTAKES

For example, quite recently I was playing a team match with an opponent who had pretty much the same level of skills and fitness as me. Now, when you play with an equal opponent, the chances are fairly high that it will be a long match, during which you will encounter many ups and downs. It's to be expected. You're not likely to win or lose very quickly.

What surprised me was that, in response to these ups and downs—especially to the downs—I found myself making the same mistakes that had dogged my game for the last fifteen years. For a while, it seemed as though nothing had changed.

We were playing on a clay court, and I'd started well, if a little luckily, winning most of the early games to put myself into a 4–1 lead in the first set. Then the other guy—let's call him Robert—began to hit his stride, returning everything that I offered. Even when I made risky shots, aiming close to the lines, Robert managed to return the ball and pass me. Whatever I did, I ended up losing the game.

In the past, my usual pattern in this kind of situation has been to respond by taking even more risks, trying to place shots deep into the corners, out of Robert's reach, and that is what I began to do.

However, as I did so, I was aware that an argument was developing inside my head. To describe this argument in legal terms, the attorney representing my decision to play high risk was saying to the judge, "Look, I'm already trying everything that I usually do and he is winning, so I have to take more chances."

My internal judge was not impressed. He objected, "You should know by now that when you play high risk you make one good shot followed by five mistakes. There's no way you can come out winning."

The attorney argued, "Well, maybe I lose, but with high risk at least I dominate the situation. I decide each point, not him. Either they are winners, or they are out of play. I don't have to work my butt off, suffering the indignity of running after every ball and still losing the points."

The judge replied, "That's true, but you are certain to lose the match and you will also lose respect for yourself, because you faked the contest, you gave up. You didn't give it your all."

I knew the judge was right.

BREAKING THE PATTERN

It takes a lot of courage for me to squarely face a situation in which I am compelled to run and run and run and still lose the point. I'm a fairly big guy and I have a fairly big first serve.

When it goes in, I expect to win the point, and I don't like the feeling of watching it come back and having to run after it, especially when I'm being outplayed. It hurts my pride.

So when Robert kept winning for seven straight games, it took a lot of awareness on my part not to go into my old pattern of switching to high-risk play.

Instead, I tried something new. I began to play a bit slower, and during the first four or five strokes of each rally I didn't try any risky shots. I hit the ball directly to Robert and he made me run. This meant accepting a lot of physical effort. I wasn't missing my shots anymore, but I had to work hard, running after his shots, giving them back to him.

I also made a point of breathing deeply into my belly. Between each exhausting rally, I would use my twenty-five-second break just to breathe into my belly, feeling my tiredness, feeling my frustration, not trying to change anything, not looking around at my teammates.

On a physical level, the breathing helped to keep my body relaxed and rejuvenated, and I was able to swing freely until the very end of the match. Even though I didn't want to run anymore, even though I didn't want to stretch anymore, I could still keep going.

On a mental and emotional level, the breathing helped me to say yes to myself and to the situation I was in. This was important, because a few years earlier, I would have been too embarrassed to play this way. My macho ego would have faulted me for not playing like a winner, for not holding my serve, for not breaking his serve, for not going for the winning shots whenever possible.

At this point, I also noticed another voice in my head, which I recognized as my meditator's ego, saying, "I thought Zennis is supposed to be graceful and playful? If you have to make so much effort, if you have to torture yourself, it can't be Zen. You must be doing something wrong."

But I wasn't being ruled by any of these voices. I didn't allow myself to escape into high-risk play, nor did I beat myself up because in this particular situation there wasn't much room to be graceful and playful.

This is why I say that the real fire test for the Zen player is in matches where there is pressure. Pressure provokes all kinds of hidden attitudes, ideas, and feelings from the subconscious part of your mind—stuff that maybe you thought you'd dealt with a long time ago; ego trips that maybe you thought you'd already transformed through some technique or workshop.

By the way, this internal Pandora's box starts to open not only when you're losing but also when you're winning. It's not just the pain, the rage, the wanting to give up that affect your play. It's also the desire to be triumphant, to show your power and skill, to say, "Now I've got him, now I'll show him who's the better player."

Winning or losing, it really doesn't matter. Under pressure, stuff will begin to surface, stuff that can get in the way of your responses to the situation as it really is, here, now, moment to moment.

As I mentioned before, I was leading 4–1 and then fell behind 5–7. Robert took the first set and also the first game of the second set, so there was a period in which he won seven games to my one. In response, I settled into a rhythm of running, running, running, hitting the ball, and sending it back.

BACK IN THE MATCH

Then Robert started missing a few shots. Actually, it's quite normal that the one who takes the initiative starts to miss. Why? Because if I'm not looking for a winner—if I'm just sending back the ball—then it's up to Robert to try and make the winning shot.

Robert started missing, and I came back in the match. Then the play entered a new phase. For a while there was a period in which each rally provided openings for both him and me to hit the winning shot, openings that perhaps neither of us would use. Sometimes after ten times back and forth, he hit a winner or I hit a winner. You could not predict who was going to take the point.

I was playing against my pattern, accepting that I was having to go the long road, staying patient, with no idea how the match would turn out. Then suddenly the second set was over and I had won it 6–4. Now everything depended on the third and final set.

Earlier, I was afraid that if the match went to three sets, the rallies would tire me out, but I actually felt more fit in the third than in the second. This was because I had accepted the situation. There was no longer a struggle going on inside my head, and so my energy was undivided, more available for the physical game.

The third set was a strange affair. After 1–1, we broke each other's serve all the way through to 6–6, completing ten service breaks in a row to reach the tie breaker. The match was still hanging in the balance. I still had no idea who was going to win.

ENTERING THE ZONE

At this crucial moment, quite unexpectedly, I entered the zone. It really had not occurred to me that in a match such as this—so challenging to my ego, so arduous for my body—

I would enter Zen space. I hadn't thought about it once during the whole match.

But suddenly it was there: a dramatic shift in gestalt, a moment in which I seemed to fall deeply inside myself through no act of will. It happened quite naturally and spontaneously, all by itself.

Everything became very silent, as if I was playing underwater. I could hear my own heartbeat, the sound of the blood pumping through my veins, while noises from the outside world seemed very far away.

Everything slowed down. As if in a slow-motion replay, I was able to watch the ball sailing slowly over the net toward me, seeing the pattern of the spinning seams, feeling my body moving into the right position to meet it, knowing the ball would hit my racket strings in exactly the right spot for a beautiful return stroke, sensing where the ball would land on my opponent's side of the net.

There was no sense of triumph or relief or excitement about being in this space, just a positive feeling each time I hit the ball, like a confirmation, again and again, that everything could happen effortlessly and poetically without any struggle on my part.

As I said before, I had been losing my serve game during the third set, but now, in the tie break, something new happened. I won my serves, but not through hitting aces. I found myself serving with less effort than before, not trying to hit a winner, just making a smooth serve that would open the rally and get the ball in play.

Normally, this would have been a hard thing for me to do. The tendency for most players, including myself, is to try to be decisive with the serve, especially the first serve, as a way of taking the initiative, of providing an edge over the opponent, especially in a tie-break situation. To serve less hard goes against the grain, but because I was in the zone, there was no internal conflict, no self-doubt. There was not even a strategic decision to play in this manner. I just found myself doing it, without even thinking about it—and it worked.

Robert mishit two balls, trying to attack the soft, incoming serves, and when we moved into the by-now-familiar rallies, I found myself playing some beautiful shots, hitting three forehand winners. The dice were rolling my way, and at 6–3 I had triple match point.

Then something happened that totally surprised me. Serving for the match, I raised my racket, but didn't take the usual windup route over the back of my head for a big swing. Instead, in a playful way, I just popped up the ball and hit it with a snap of my wrist, rather like executing an overhead smash, and I was surprised to see that I had hit the only clean ace of the third set.

LUCK, TACTICS, GOD OR . . . ?

I had a very big grin when that happened, and I have to say, as I jogged to the net to shake hands with Robert, that there was no great feeling of having pulled off a victory through my own ingenuity and prowess. Rather, I felt as if somebody or something did it for me—won the match for me. An energy greater than my own had taken over and played through me. All I did was to get out of the way and let it happen.

"I felt I was more lucky than you today," I said, seeing how disappointed Robert was to have lost his first match for his new team. He said nothing, just shrugged and silently shook my hand.

There was a surprise in store for me when I started to discuss the match with the guys from my team. They were convinced that I had been in control throughout the match, using very deliberate tactics, while in my own reality I had no feeling—during the whole match—of being in command of the situation. I had no notion who was going to win, except during Robert's seven-game run when I didn't feel I could catch up with him.

Nor did my fellow teammates sense my embarrassment at having to run around the court, chasing balls and missing shots in front of their critical eyes. My sense of wounded pride was entirely my own creation and projection.

By the way, this feeling I had as the match ended—that somebody did it for me—is quite common at all levels of tennis, when a player has given his total effort. The sensation is that some energy, some higher power or force, is working through you, carrying your game beyond your normal range of skill or effort.

When a player has an experience of this kind, it is tempting to label it in terms of conventional religious belief. For example, Michael Chang calls it the Lord Jesus, and there is a substantial number of born-again Christians on the tennis circuit who attribute their victories to Jesus Christ.

This is understandable but in my view misguided. It turns a beautiful, energetic experience into a religious concept. It also creates all kinds of ideological difficulties, because there is an unfortunate tendency, present in almost all religions, to claim exclusive rights to spiritual truth. Jesus, as every Christian knows, is the only begotten Son of God and therefore the only Savior.

In terms of winning a tennis match, this creates problems. After all, if a Christian wins today and a Buddhist wins tomorrow, then what happened to the supreme powers of Jesus? Was he taking a day off, or is Gautama Buddha a better coach? And what if an atheist wins? Has God deserted the faithful?

Zen has the wisdom not to label the mysterious. The function of Zen is to help people experience such inner states, not to categorize them. Zen also makes it clear that the responsibility lies in your own hands. You have the crucial part to play.

As many mystics have pointed out, the universal principle, the cosmic consciousness—call it what you will—is always available to pour its energy through any human being, regardless of his or her spiritual beliefs. You just need to be open, in tune, in resonance with this energy. It's basically up to you.

Nor is it necessarily true that this feeling of being in tune is going to create victory. When I walked off the court with Robert, I was very much aware that I could have done everything that I did, going against my old patterns, going the long road, even entering the zone, and still lost the match.

ZEN IS CONCERNED WITH YOU

Zen is not concerned with victory but with you. Victory may happen as a by-product, because naturally your game will be raised to new heights when you enter such beautiful spaces, but the real thing is how you played, how you responded to the situation.

Did you play mechanically and habitually or freshly and spontaneously? Did you try to impose a preconceived strategy on the match, or did you tune yourself to the reality on the court, accepting each new situation as it developed and adapting your play accordingly?

As I have already indicated, match play is a fire test for the Zen player because it creates pressure in which many old behavior patterns will be provoked. The challenge is to see if you can play your best tennis while these buttons are being pushed, while all the old feelings are being stirred. In this way, it's a reality check for the meditator. It's a mirror and a magnifying glass in one.

If you are overly competitive, it will show; if you are too serious, it will show; if you are whining and complaining, it will show; if you have no confidence, it will show; and if you have a relaxed twinkle in your eye, it will also show—maybe not to anyone else but certainly to you.

The essential quality that goes with Zen onto the court is being detached enough to notice what is happening, both inside and out. One match like this gives you food for thought for quite a while.

By the way, I am not suggesting that the path I took in my match with Robert has any value beyond the game itself. It is simply one example and, I hope, an encouragement for you to look at your own habits, your own patterns, and see how they influence your ability to be a Zennis player.

RECOGNIZING THE ZONE

I would like to conclude this chapter by talking a little more about the zone and about some of the confirmatory signs that can help a player understand that he or she has entered this space. Recognizing these signs can help you to stay relaxed, allowing it to happen without making much fuss, without spoiling the whole experience by getting excited or worried.

Even a few years ago, it would have been risky for an athlete or sportsman to talk about the zone, to mention the kind of mystical experiences that happen when they play at their very best. Such talk would have seemed a bit weird, a bit too far out of the accepted parameters of conversation.

Nowadays there is more shared understanding, more agreement that such spaces exist. In fact, one tennis racket company even used the term *zone* in a television commercial to promote its product. In addition, there are whole books devoted to descriptions of such spaces attained by outstanding athletes at peak moments of their careers.

For example, the great Brazilian soccer player, Pele, has shared an experience of a world championship match in which he entered a space or state and did not even see the defending players of the opposing team. He saw only the gaps, the openings, through which he could move with the ball toward the goal, and in this way he scored three goals. Nobody could touch him.

One important aspect of the zone is that it cannot be achieved through effort or willpower. In this sense, it's similar to the phenomenon that you experience each night of falling asleep. You can't make yourself fall asleep—that's a sure way to stay awake. You can only lie down, relax, and wait for sleep to come.

It's the same with the zone. If you start thinking about it, if you try to somehow manage it, you will succeed only in avoiding it. But you can prepare the ground for the zone, maximizing the chances for it to happen.

For me, the key is that you need to reach a space of high physical intensity. When you have given everything, when you have burned through layers and layers of energy, when you don't know where you will get the energy to play the next point, then you have a chance to suddenly move into Zen space.

Sometimes, too, the zone occurs when the mind has given up the struggle for victory. You have been doing your best to win, trying one strategy, then another, but still you are trailing behind and there comes a point where your mind simply does not know what to do anymore. The temptation, at this point, is to slip into an attitude of defeat. But if you stay open and innocent, not judging this space, not condemning yourself, the chances are that a different door will open and you will enter the zone.

In my experience, what is required at such moments is a feeling of trust—trust in yourself. You are losing, your mind wants to start criticizing, nagging, and complaining, but instead you trust yourself enough to ignore these comments, staying in the present moment, here and now, not knowing what is going to happen next.

If you can do this, there is a good possibility that you will suddenly find yourself entering the most exquisite space available in the game of tennis. One of the main reasons why people enter the zone so rarely is that they are too identified with the chattering of their own minds. They do not know the art of standing to one side, watching the stream of thoughts, not getting caught up in any of them. This art is acquired through meditation. The more you meditate, the better your chances of hitting the zone.

Even so, it's not possible to predict when a zone experience will happen. For example, you can find yourself in the zone right at the beginning of a match, without any prior physical intensity. This has happened to me on several occasions when I have just been through some deep emotional experience away from the world of tennis, such as the death of a close friend or the end or beginning of a love relationship.

Coming to the court in such a condition, I did not have any attachment to the outcome of the match. I wanted to enjoy a game, to play well, but I really didn't care about winning or tactics or what anyone thought about my performance. There were far more important things in life than hitting a ball over a net. Then, just starting to play, I would slip into the Zen space.

ZONE CHARACTERISTICS

Perhaps by now some readers are wondering whether they have experienced this space and how to recognize it. To help you answer this question, here are some of the signs and the characteristics of being in the zone.

- You see the ball as bigger. The yellow ball traveling toward you may seem twice as big as it usually does.

- The oncoming ball seems to travel more slowly, giving you much more time to respond. As I have said, watching the ball can seem as if you are watching a slow-motion replay, but your reflexes are at normal speed.

- You have a heightened sense of awareness, especially during the last moments before the ball hits the strings of the racket. You experience the ball slowing down even more and you may notice details: that parts of the ball are in bright light and parts are in shade, that the spinning seams create a pattern.

- At the moment of impact, when you hit the ball, you may see dust spraying out like a ring around the ball.

Also, the ball may seem to stay longer on your racket, hitting that sweet spot right in the middle where the strings can give their best response.

° You know beforehand where the ball is going to go, before your opponent has even made his shot. It's like a sixth sense for the direction in which the ball will move.

° You experience a quietness inside yourself, as if playing underwater, almost as if your ears have changed direction from outside to inside. You may hear your own pulse, your own heartbeat. Outside noises seem miles away.

° There is no mental planning, no strategic thinking, but a natural feeling of rhythm in your play. For example, you don't deliberately try and wrong-foot your opponent or play to a weak backhand, but you will find yourself sending the ball to those places on the court where it may happen anyway.

° You play your very best tennis in this space. It seems like a quantum leap from how you usually play. Everything seems very easy, effortless, and you wonder how you could ever have missed a ball. Every shot brings a deep sense of satisfaction—not because it wins a point, but for the sheer intensity of feeling and fulfillment that it provides.

Almost every tennis player has glimpses of the zone, even if it is only for a few moments, and these are the beautiful experiences that draw people back into the game again and again. It's a feeling of magic, of meditation in which people are able to receive a glimpse of their true nature.

It should be remembered, too, that there are sensitive players, like John McEnroe in the eighties and Ilie Nastase in the seventies, who can detect when an opponent is moving into the zone. That's the moment when they will stage a disruption, creating incidents or throwing temper tantrums in an effort to prevent it from happening.

These provocative characters aren't content with experiencing the zone for themselves. They may not do it consciously, but they are out to destroy your zone experience as a way of ensuring their own victory. When you meet such players, this can be the ultimate challenge: to stay in your center, to stay in the zone, when they are doing everything possible to throw you out of it.

Such challenges mirror the way a man of Zen moves in the world: staying centered in himself while surrounded by a thousand and one distractions of every imaginable kind.

Do You Mind?

An English tourist was hiking through the Hindu Kush mountains. The weather was hot, there was no shade, and the hiker was eager to find a place to rest for a while and recover his strength. Turning a corner on the mountain path, he saw an ancient sage sitting under a tree on the hillside. Putting down his backpack, the hiker approached the sage and asked, "Do you mind if I join you?"

"In the first place," replied the sage, "I don't have a mind."

11
Stepping Outside Your Paradigm

Some years ago I turned on the TV to watch live coverage of the U.S. Open, but the matches were delayed because of rain, and the commentators were obliged to fill the vacuum with discussion and personal anecdotes. Among those interviewed was Rudi Berger, a well-known umpire on the professional tennis circuit, a man who travels with the international caravan of players, week in and week out.

Among the questions put to Berger was, predictably enough, the following: "What was the most unusual moment in your long experience of umpiring matches?"

I couldn't believe my ears when I heard Berger mention my name.

He answered, "The most unusual moment was during a match between Peter Spang from Germany and Shankar Perkis from Israel."

Berger went on to describe the incident, which I remembered very clearly. It happened during a close match in a minor European tournament. The score was 5–5 in the third and final set, and 15–15 in the eleventh game, with Perkis serving. At that moment, for the fourth time, the strings of his racket broke.

It happens occasionally that a professional player breaks the strings of four rackets during a match. It never happened to me, but I always carried five or six rackets with me in case of freak accidents.

Perkis walked to the side of the court to check his bag, but there were no more rackets. He had brought only four with him. He stood by the side of the court, not knowing what to do.

Berger leaned over from his umpire seat and said, "Mr. Perkis, please continue to play."

Perkis replied that he had no more rackets and stood passively by his bench, as if he had given up the idea of continuing the match.

The strange thing was that Perkis did not try to get a racket from another source. When I offered him one of mine, he refused. Nor did he ask anybody in the crowd, several of whom were tennis players.

After about three minutes of a bizarre pause, with Perkis just standing there, with nothing actually happening, Berger had to disqualify him for not continuing the match and declare me the winner.

Relating the incident on television, Berger said it was the only time in his umpiring career that he had to disqualify a player in such an odd manner.

To me, the incident is significant because it shows how a psychological barrier can interfere with a player's performance. For Perkis, the match was over because his personal supply of rackets was finished. In his mind, the unanticipated situation of no personal rackets translated as the belief that "I can't play anymore."

Additional elements in the equation, such as the availability of other players' rackets and the fact that Perkis had a good chance of winning the match if he continued, seemingly had no influence.

PARADIGMS: SHAPING YOUR THINKING

The preceding story is an example of how our thinking is shaped by paradigms, and that is why I begin this chapter with it.

"Paradigm" is a scientific expression meaning a set of rules or beliefs that establish limits or borders, giving shape and definition to a particular idea, theory, or hypothesis. Paradigms are important in the field of scientific investigation because when you define the nature of a particular inquiry, you also tend to determine the outcome of that inquiry.

I am no physicist, but I can provide a crude example of how this works. Let us say that you are looking for a tiny subatomic particle called a snark. In looking for your snark, you have already formed certain ideas about it: where it may be found, how it may behave, how it may be detected, what its function may be.

Such ideas are inevitable; otherwise, how in the first place would you know that your snark exists? Without them, you would not even be able to begin your investigation.

These ideas create your paradigm, defining the territory and circumstances of your investigation. And these ideas also make you, the scientist, part of the investigation, because it is you who are defining the boundaries of your inquiry.

During your investigation, you gather information about the snark. Naturally, you will try to fit this information into the paradigm that you have already created. Moreover, if you are not careful, you will probably emphasize information that supports your paradigm and discard information that does not fit with it.

In reality, the snark may be entirely different. It may not exist within your paradigm at all. Or it may exist only partially within your paradigm. But until somebody comes along with a better paradigm and proves you wrong, you are likely to remain convinced that you have the correct ideas about it, supported by the evidence you have found.

In other words, what you believe tends to influence what you find. This is one of the greatest contributions of modern physics: the discovery that the way you approach an investigation—the boundaries you establish and the limits you set—also tends to determine the outcome. And the same is true about life. The ideas you form about your life are going to strongly influence how you experience it.

A COSTLY BLIND SPOT

Understanding paradigms has become a critical factor in commerce and business, because corporate planners realize that what is perceived as the function of a particular corporation is going to determine the future of that corporation. In this context, a bad paradigm can cost billions of dollars.

In the 1960s, the Swiss watchmaking industry controlled 90 percent of the world market in watches. Their main product was the tried-and-tested mechanical watch. By the late

1970s, the Swiss controlled only 15 percent of the market and had been forced to lay off about 50,000 people in their watchmaking industry. For a small country like Switzerland, the impact was almost catastrophic.

What had happened? The liquid quartz watch had flooded the world market.

From the perspective of understanding the impact of paradigms, the most interesting thing about this revolution was the fact that the Swiss themselves developed the liquid quartz watch. Pioneering Swiss researchers had already presented it as a commercial possibility, but nobody in the watchmaking establishment was able to recognize its potential, not to speak of the danger it represented. They simply dismissed it as a crazy idea. It did not fit into the paradigm of traditional watchmaking. It didn't have the quality, the class, or the craftsmanship to which they were accustomed.

They did not even protect the discovery, so when the idea of the liquid quartz watch was presented at an international watchmakers' congress, the rights were bought by Seiko of Japan and Texas Instruments of the United States, who both made a fortune.

A PROFITABLE INNOVATION

Similar things happen in commerce all the time. Hence, many corporations now encourage paradigm pioneers to work inside their organizations, questioning the basic assumptions on which the business is built, exploring unorthodox options, lessening the risk of being overtaken on the blind side by a more innovative company.

In Germany, the giant international oil company British Petroleum now makes more money through its gas station supermarkets than through the sale of oil and gas. This is a paradigm shift. One can guess that, when the idea was first proposed to BP's executives, the more conservative-minded of them thought it strange. Why should a successful oil company also become a store chain?

But the idea was brilliant. With its network of gas stations, BP already had a functioning infrastructure in every village, town, and city in the country. Most people simply saw these places as gas stations, but the paradigm pioneers saw them as retail outlets and asked: What else can sell here besides car-related products? For BP and also for the German public—especially on Sundays when all other shops are closed—the idea proved a blessing.

WHY CHANGE A WINNER?

Many tennis players remember the time when all rackets were made of wood and were a standard size. In the beginning of the 1980s, the first aluminum oversized tennis racket entered the market, but it was not taken seriously. It was laughed about. Then, slowly, a few professionals started to practice with it, adapting their styles of play to the new racket and discovering that it could produce impressive results.

At this early stage, the giants of the tennis racket industry could have begun development programs to produce their own versions of the new type of racket, first in aluminum, then in the graphite model that succeeded it.

But many resisted the idea. The Belgium firm of Donnay, for example, had Bjorn Borg under contract to promote its wooden rackets. Borg, a great champion, had won all of his five Wimbledon titles with a wooden Donnay racket. Why change a winning product? Donnay's managers were convinced that the future of tennis rackets would always be in wood and dismissed the new metal rackets as a passing fashion.

The result? They ended up with millions of wooden rackets in their warehouses and narrowly avoided bankruptcy.

GRAPHITE RACKETS CHANGE THE GAME

The game of tennis also experienced a paradigm shift, moving parallel with the advancement in racket materials. For decades, tennis had been dominated by players who were gifted in consistency, endurance, and finesse. Now, suddenly, the game became ruled by power, because the bigger, harder graphite rackets allowed everybody to play more powerfully.

If you wanted to win in a changing tennis world, you needed to have killer shots—fast, hard, and accurate—especially with your serve and forehand. Even if a player lacked certain skills and techniques, he could usually beat more versatile players providing he could hit hard enough. Thus a heavy hitter like Jim Courier could beat a gifted player like John McEnroe.

Now, however, the game is shifting once more. The very best players, such as Pete Sampras and Andre Agassi, have the ability to mix power and touch, blending killer shots with artistry.

Sampras, for example, will sometimes hit twenty aces and twenty touch volleys in a match. One stroke may be hard, the next may just caress the ball.

Agassi does not hit many aces, but when he is in form, he can blast dozens of return winners, showing his sensitivity of touch with awesome cross-court angles, hitting balls that bounce short behind the net, pulling his opponents far outside the court in an effort to retrieve them.

The two men represent a new paradigm—the latest to influence world-class tennis—that mixes power and finesse.

More generally, it can be said that the sport of tennis, and everybody who is involved in it, is shaped by paradigms that establish boundaries and limitations. These boundaries are not necessarily bad. For example, fair play is a paradigm. It creates limits to prevent players from indulging in off-the-wall behavior, such as physically assaulting each other, and in this way establishes a context in which the game can happen.

PERSONAL PARADIGMS: SHAPING YOUR LIFE

But it is not just sports, corporations, and scientific inquiry that are influenced by paradigms. People are, too. Every individual has, during his or her lifetime, created a set of boundaries and beliefs that influence the way the world is perceived.

One of the easiest ways to see people's personal paradigms in action is to note what happens when they want to eat out and are trying to decide which restaurant to visit. For example, I have a friend, Veronica, who for years would eat only Italian. Although I am fond of sushi, I could never manage to persuade Veronica to try Japanese food, or, indeed, any cultural culinary style save the one to be found in Little Italy. She knew she liked pasta, so pasta it invariably turned out to be.

Then Veronica had to go to Tokyo and other Japanese cities on a business trip. She was invited out to dinner by her hosts and, of course, nobody even dreamed of taking her to an Italian restaurant. Out of courtesy, Veronica had to eat

Japanese food, and by the time she came back to New York, a major transformation had taken place. Veronica has discovered that she likes Japanese food. It was just a personal paradigm—"When I go out I must eat Italian"—that was preventing her from recognizing the fact that she could eat and enjoy something other than Italian food.

For people who are interested in self-discovery and personal growth, paradigms are fascinating and helpful because once you understand the paradigm in which you are living, you already have the potential to go beyond it. The fact that you are aware of your paradigm gives you the ability to step outside it, creating more choice and more possibilities.

PARADIGMS ON THE COURT

Now, let us see how personal paradigms work on the tennis court. Recently, I was working with a forty-two-year-old named Arthur, and I noticed that whenever I gave him a fast ball, he would respond by hitting hard, trying to return the ball to me even faster than I had sent it to him.

Sometimes it worked, and the ball zipped past me for a winner, but most of the time his aim was too erratic, and he lost many points.

I asked him, "Arthur, are you aware of how you respond to my hard shots?"

He shook his head, puzzled.

So we played on, because I wanted him to come to the realization himself. After a few more minutes, he understood his pattern of fast returns.

"Why do you do it?" I asked. "Do you have any special reason? Is this the smartest way to deal with my hard shots?"

Arthur thought for a moment.

"Well, it's definitely not the smartest way, because I miss a lot of balls," he replied.

I asked him if he would be willing to stop playing for a few minutes, sit down by the side of the court, close his eyes, and reflect on the issue. He agreed.

After about five minutes, Arthur opened his eyes and started to talk.

"It feels a bit like a masculinity trip," he ventured. "Something about my image, about not wanting to look weak. If you challenge me with a fast ball, then I've got to match your power."

I felt Arthur was touching on something significant, because I have noticed the same tendency with many men.

I asked Arthur to tell me more, and he continued, "It's a feeling of wanting to be respected, of not wanting to be insulted. If I don't hit the ball as hard as you, then I'm left with a feeling of inferiority, and I don't like that at all."

It became obvious to both of us that Arthur was stuck in a paradigm called "When I'm challenged I have to display my power."

Inside this paradigm, there was no possibility for him to simply return the ball, keeping it in play, waiting for a better chance, or to respond with a lob, or to give me a slice. He had only one option: to slam the ball back. Even though eight out of ten balls were hitting the net or landing beyond the lines, Arthur felt he had to keep repeating the same stroke.

I discovered a similar paradigm with Barry, a younger man who booked a lesson with me in order to improve his return of serve. This is the moment when you have to deal with the fastest, most powerful ball your opponent can give you, when you have less time than in any other situation—

unless, perhaps, somebody drills an overhead smash at you while you are standing at the net.

Barry responded to my serves by trying to swing at them with even more force than I was using, and was miss-hitting a high percentage. Mostly they struck the frame of his racket.

Like Arthur, in response to power, Barry was locked in a paradigm called "I have to be equally powerful."

When this became obvious, I asked Barry to explore stepping out of the paradigm and creating different responses to a fast serve.

"How about if I just put my racket here, like this, and let the ball hit the middle of my strings?" he suggested.

"Let's try it," I replied.

Barry experimented for a while, returning the ball without using any backswing, simply blocking my serves. He quickly became enthusiastic about the new strategy because he stopped miss-hitting. He was amazed at how easily he could return a ball using its own power, without adding extra force.

I supported his discovery with a few tips: indicating that he should relax his knees and belly so that he could feel that he was absorbing the power of the oncoming ball, taking it into his body and sending it back. As a result, he experienced an almost effortless way of playing, discovering that being a good tennis player is not just a matter of muscle power. It's also about flexibility of response.

Even at the top levels of tennis, you can sometimes get away with a blocking return shot. Players are so accustomed to speed and power that a slow, low shot tends to throw them off balance. That's one way to beat a good server: he is running to the net, expecting to volley a hard return, and instead you slide in a soft, low ball at his feet.

PLEASING THE COACH

One paradigm that I have often noted with women players—especially at the stage when they are not yet self-confident—is that they want to please the coach. Men also have this tendency, but not to the same degree.

For example, I was playing with Anna, a gifted young athlete who had a natural ability to retrieve the ball. We played long rallies in which Anna managed to return almost every ball, but I could sense that she was not really enjoying herself, not playing freely and spontaneously, not allowing herself to take risks.

After about thirty minutes I asked Anna if she was enjoying the lesson. She immediately said yes, but when she saw that I was waiting for something more, she added: "I guess I was expecting more instruction."

"Instruction in what?" I asked.

"Well, for example, in hitting a few winners, not just batting the ball back over the net like I do," she replied.

"Why don't you just do it? Why wait for me to give you permission?" I asked.

As our conversation progressed, Anna started to uncover her paradigm. She realized that she was playing safe because she didn't want to disappoint me.

"How do you not disappoint a coach?" I asked.

"By keeping the ball in play, getting it over the net, hitting inside the lines," she replied.

"In other words, by not taking risks," I suggested.

"That's right. What can be more disappointing to a coach than to see his student miss a ball?" she replied.

"I'd like you to show me how you would play if you didn't give a damn for my approval," I said.

"All right!" exclaimed Anna, excited by the possibility.

There was an immediate change in Anna's game. She hit with more power, more variety. She took risks. She laughed, she screamed, she cussed, she became totally alive and in the process played some great tennis. All these vital energies had been bottled up when she was trying to do it right for the coach.

WHAT CAN BE LEARNED?

As I see it, applying the concept of paradigms in tennis is a useful method of creating distance between you and your behavior patterns, so that you can understand that these patterns are not you. For example, you may be playing in an overly macho way, and this may be spoiling your game, but now you can say, "It's not really me, it's just a paradigm." This makes it easier to let go of your pattern and change your game.

In daily life, there is not usually much space for people to step outside their paradigms and explore new ideas, new aspects of themselves. Family members, friends, colleagues, employers, staff . . . all expect a certain kind of predictable behavior from you. They may even become upset if you do not fulfill their expectations and start to behave in an unorthodox manner.

For people caught in such paradigms there is great potential, freedom, and creativity in stepping onto the tennis court. It can be an arena of self-discovery. You can leave your paradigms in the locker room, along with your office clothes, and explore new sides of yourself, gaining insights that have the power to transform the quality of your life.

For example, you can learn to become more playful on

the court. You can experiment with being relaxed under pressure while remaining centered and alert. You can find new ways to work with partners, to deal with opponents, to experience defeat and victory, loss and gain, to cope with uncertainty and fast-changing situations. You can understand what paradigms are shaping you, setting limits to your attitudes and behavior.

SOME COMMON PARADIGMS

Here are some common paradigms that apply to tennis and also to life in general:

- ° Don't make a fool of yourself.
- ° Don't try something that you haven't done before.
- ° Try to look good, on top of the situation, no matter what happens.
- ° If you're winning it's okay to play fair, but if you're losing your calls get tougher.
- ° In order to improve, you have to practice a lot.
- ° To show emotion is a sign of weakness and makes you a loser.
- ° Fooling around is a waste of time.
- ° Hard work is the only way to get ahead.

These paradigms can be explored on the tennis court, and the resulting discoveries can be applied to any dimension of life.

A LIMITING BELIEF

Let's look at one of these paradigms in action on the court. For example, "Don't try something that you haven't done before," or, putting it another way, "Stick with what you know, especially if it's paying dividends."

Ralph is a middle-aged tennis enthusiast with plenty of free time, and for a few years he really played a lot, but recently I don't see him so much on the court. He is suffering from tennis blues. He can't get past certain players in the club rankings and, what is worse, some new players are starting to overtake him.

His problem is most visible when he plays Karl, a colleague with whom he feels very competitive. Whenever they play together, he really wants to win, because he knows that later on, in the bar, it's going to be the talk with the other guys: who won this time, how the game went, and so on.

About a year ago, when Ralph and Karl started to play together, Ralph was almost always the winner because he had more experience and more skills. He was good at keeping the ball in play, he pushed forehands consistently to his opponent's weaker backhand, employed a limited but effective backhand slice, and could rely on a high lob when Karl tried to attack at the net.

At that time, Ralph was almost always in a confident mood and liked to talk between points and games, saying things like "I'm hot today, you have no chance," or else he would give advice to Karl as to how he could play better.

Now, one year later, the situation has changed. Ralph still plays the same game, with the same basic skills, but Karl has improved dramatically. Through losing a lot of matches, he felt motivated to look at his game and develop new strokes and responses.

For example, Karl knows now that he can attack Ralph's backhand without much risk, because the response will probably be a lob and he can already start running into position to smash a winner.

The scores now look as bad for Ralph as they did for Karl a year ago. In frustration, Ralph told me that he's getting bored with tennis, and that "My backhand is letting me down."

I disagreed. "Your backhand is fine," I told him. "It's the same as a year ago when you were so excited to have that stroke in your repertoire. But you settled for a few wins and stopped developing your game. You lost the quality of being curious, unlike your friend Karl."

I asked Ralph, "What do you need in order to match Karl's improvement?"

Ralph's response was clear: "I need to develop a backhand passing shot and I need to be more creative with the ball when I take the initiative. Simply pushing balls back over the net doesn't do it anymore."

In practical terms, when Ralph steps out of the paradigm called "stick with what you know," he might usefully develop a backhand topspin and take a few coaching lessons to see what other strokes he can learn. For him, the exercise Red Light, Green Light, mentioned in chapter 4, would be a helpful method of developing a more creative style.

A BEAUTIFUL OPPORTUNITY

My main point here is that, while playing tennis, we all have a beautiful opportunity to see our paradigms in action and explore stepping outside them. It's a mirror of life. For example, it's okay to enjoy a winning streak, as Ralph did for the past year, but it's also good to understand that nothing stays the same for long.

Life is a river of energy whose nature is continuously changing. We have to learn the art of flowing with the current, understanding each new situation as it arises, and responding accordingly. This is a problem for people who have fixed ideas, because they are trying to build a dam across a fast-moving river. Once you acquire the knack of recognizing fixed ideas as paradigms, you regain the ability to swim with the current.

EXPERIMENTING WITH NEW ROLES

In concluding this chapter, I'd like to suggest some exercises that can help you explore the territory beyond your current paradigm.

First of all, think of a player, either on the international scene or in your local tennis circle, who reminds you of your own style of play. It might be Michael Chang, Andre Agassi, Monica Seles, or Steffi Graf. This will help you to become clear about the paradigm you are currently in.

The next step is to think of a player who is farthest from your style. For example, if you tend to be a serve-and-volley player, like Becker or Sampras, then choose a player who relies on consistency and endurance, like Thomas Muster or Bjorn Borg. If you are a baseline player like Muster, then choose someone who plays the net a lot, like Sampras. In other words, go to the opposite extreme.

For women, if you are a player who likes to take the initiative, like Steffi Graf or Martina Navratilova, then choose a counterpuncher like Arancha Sanchez or Chris Evert.

Once you have a clear idea of the player who is least like you, I invite you to go onto the tennis court and put your wholehearted enthusiasm into playing like this person. Drop your old of idea of how to play tennis, and move into the style of the person you have selected.

This can be a fascinating and entertaining way of expanding your existing paradigm. Even if you discover that you are happier with your old game, the exercise will improve your skills and you will play better, because a good opponent will in any case force you into these unfamiliar roles at times.

Even Graf, when she plays a strong opponent, has to be a counterpuncher sometimes. Even Sanchez has to take the initiative occasionally if she wants to win.

In addition to experimenting with styles of play, you can also explore different personality types. For example, if you tend to be a hot-tempered, explosive character, like McEnroe, you can try being cool and detached like Sampras. On the other hand, if you are the introverted type, you can try being wildly extroverted, shouting and complaining when you miss a shot, cheering when you hit a winner. No role is necessarily better. You're simply using the court as a playful zone for experimenting, becoming more flexible.

CHANGING THE RULES

One thing I liked about the 1996 Olympics in Atlanta was the introduction of beach volleyball, which is played outdoors on sand, with two players on either side of the net.

This sport was created by stepping outside the paradigm that says volleyball has to be five against five.

In the same spirit, I invite you to experiment with playing three against three on the tennis court. It can be a lot of fun, especially if you allow the ball to bounce twice and be hit twice on each side of the net before being returned.

You can also make the net higher by running a cord parallel to the net, three feet above it, playing tennis with a six-foot barrier.

You can play a match using one serve instead of two. In this way the serve becomes a device to open up a rally, rather than a weapon and point-winner in itself.

These are all ways to step outside the paradigms that govern the game of tennis, ways to explore not only the game but also your own attitudes.

For the Zen tennis player, the essence of working with paradigms is this: You are not what you think you are. You are not confined to your current identity, beliefs, and attitudes. You are much more, and you can explore this uncharted territory by stepping outside old paradigms and creating new ones for yourself.

These new paradigms can be your very own work of art, and for this purpose the tennis court makes a wonderful artist's studio.

The Short Path

A seeker came to a Zen mystic and asked for instruction. The mystic invited him to join a group of disciples who were practicing various methods of meditation and self-awareness.

"How long have they been practicing?" inquired the newcomer.

"Some for a few weeks, some for months, some for several years," replied the mystic.

The newcomer shook his head impatiently. "Does it have to take so long?" he asked. "Can't you give me a method that will bring immediate illumination?"

"Of course, if that is what you wish," replied the mystic. "There is a short, simple, and very direct method. It is simply this: that from sunset tonight until sunrise tomorrow you should not think of red monkeys."

"I will do it!" cried the newcomer excitedly.

"Come to me tomorrow and report your progress," said the mystic.

After a night of sheer self-torture, during which he was unable to think of anything except red monkeys, the newcomer came back the following day and humbly asked for permission to join the group of disciples.

12
Creating a Zennis Support Group

Why play tennis? For me, the answer is that I like to move my body; I like to feel vitally alive, to challenge myself, to play with courage, to interact with other people in a heartful and playful way, and to have the feeling that I am still growing, still learning about myself, about others, and about the game of tennis.

If you also like to play tennis this way, the best way to make it happen is to create a group of players who share the same values as yourself: a Zennis support group, a gathering of friends who come together to play as a path to self-awareness.

When creating such a group, it's useful to see it as a structure that stands on four pillars: sharing, playing, meditating, and celebrating.

SHARING

When you start looking inward through the window of Zennis, you soon notice how much is happening in your inner world, how many facets there are to your psyche, how many mysteries and unsolved puzzles you come across on your journey of self-exploration.

Up to now, your tendency may have been to push away any strange, unfamiliar, or unpleasant experiences that bubbled up during or after a match. Now, these same experiences, these feelings, these insights, can become your treasure box. They can be doorways to greater self-understanding, deeper self-knowledge.

For most people it is helpful to talk about these experiences, giving them shape and color through communication. Naturally, in order to do this, someone is needed to listen, so that a dance of creative expression can happen between speaking and listening. Often, people are surprised by what they have to say when they start to share their inner process with another person.

It's not so much that you will get useful feedback from the listener, although this can certainly happen as a by-product. It's more that you feel challenged by the other person's loving and listening presence to dig deeper into yourself, to find words that can shed light on the things you want to share.

The Zennis support group provides an atmosphere in which you can show yourself authentically and honestly. Each person feels encouraged to step forward and share what has happened while playing. It is a place where you don't need to wear social masks. It can be called a holy place, in the sense that the underlying purpose of the group is to make people more whole—to bring people closer to their own buddha nature.

In the beginning, it is best to limit the size of a Zennis support group to between three and eight people, as this provides plenty of opportunity for everyone to participate during a single meeting. Bigger groups tend to create an imbalance whereby a few articulate people dominate the sharing process, while those who feel more nervous and insecure remain silent.

A Moderator

It's helpful to have somebody who is a moderator, and this job can rotate on a weekly basis, with everybody taking a turn. The moderator makes sure everybody has the opportunity to speak and that other members are attentive as a support for whoever is speaking.

This requires a certain maturity from all the participants, because if you are too full of yourself, with what you want to say, then you cannot really listen to anyone else. If you have a full cup, no fresh tea can be poured into it, so the challenge for each participant is to become empty again and again, and therefore open to the new.

From this perspective, it's wise to start the meeting with a short meditation. For example, it can be helpful to begin with five minutes of gibberish—talking any kind of nonsense—followed by five minutes of silence. The gibberish meditation has been described in detail in chapter 6.

The moderator needs to be aware that it's a delicate art not to let meetings turn into philosophical discussions. From time to time he may need to remind people not to generalize but to share real, pragmatic, current experiences. In addition, he needs to ensure that different realities and perspectives are allowed to stand next to each other, that no one standpoint needs to win over any other.

Many times, a person who starts to share his or her on-court experience will begin by saying something like, "I always make double faults when I have a chance to win. I can't believe that I am still doing it in match play after the good results I have in practice. "

This is a good place to start. Then the moderator can help the person move a little deeper by asking questions like, "What's happening inside when you stand at the serve line?"

Slowly the answers will shift from explanations like, "My technique is not good enough," to "I want to beat so-and-so and I am experiencing fear of failure."

This becomes an opportunity for other participants to share similar experiences. The one who kicked off the conversation can relax while the others talk, and maybe he can look a bit deeper at the origins of his fear—in what other life situations he has come across this kind of feeling, where in the past he has had similar experiences.

The Right Attitude: Open Curiosity

By the way, the atmosphere in which these sensitive issues are shared does not need to become heavy, depressive, or melancholy. Of course, when something painful or embarrassing is being shared, there is bound to be intensity and depth, but participants should steer away from the tendency to slide into the confession booth. You are not asking forgiveness for your sins. You are not getting down on yourself for being inadequate. You are not undergoing therapy. You are looking, with the open curiosity of a scientist, at something that is happening inside you in order to grow in freedom and understanding.

Another tendency to be avoided in such meetings is to try and keep things light and humorous by being wittily sarcastic. It's common among sports jocks that when someone starts sharing a personal experience, touching a vulnerable place, there is an immediate sarcastic response from another team member or player. The chances are that this person also feels vulnerable, but does not want to admit it. The use of sarcasm, even in fun, is a way of playing safe. In the context of a Zennis support group, it prevents people from establishing mutual trust.

When conducted in the right way, group sharing creates a dynamic, positive energy among the participants. People start to feel expanded and uplifted. This is because, in revealing and sharing experiences that would otherwise remain secret, tremendous energies are getting freed within you, making you feel more vital and alive. Each person's contribution adds to the collective group energy.

One of the keys to steering a Zennis support group in the right direction is making sure the group's participants are contributing, sharing, and exploring together in a supportive way; then the whole group will feel energized. There will be difficult moments, flat moments, moments of not knowing what will happen next, but the general atmosphere will be one of rising together on a wave of energy generated by the sharing process.

In addition, the fact that your friends know about your so-called weaknesses and your sensitive spots can be a major support while you face your internal demons. This may feel a bit uncomfortable at first, because we live in a culture where the myth of the lonesome cowboy still has fascination, where the basic attitude—especially among men—is that when things get tough, you don't show your vulnerability or ask for help but try to deal with everything in silent isolation.

For me, the opposite is true. It takes a lot of courage to expose your true feelings to other people.

Examples of Sharing

At this point, I'd like to give a few illustrations of how people have helped themselves by sharing on-court experiences in a support group.

Renee, a young woman from Montreal, complained that she would always wait until the last moment to take her racket back and prepare for a return shot. She would do it so late that often she had no chance to meet the ball in front of her body, and as a result, she frequently mishit.

In the process of talking about this habit with the group, she was asked, "Is your tendency to prepare late for things confined to the tennis court, or is it more general?

At first, Renee said it was only a tennis-related habit, but a little later, after the conversation had moved in another direction, she suddenly began to laugh in an embarrassed sort of way and told the group, "It's not true what I said. There is a life pattern that I'm beginning to see here. You know, I hate making decisions. I always wait until the very last moment and then often decide from panic rather than from clarity. My fear is that if I don't leave all the options open, I will be disadvantaged."

Vince, another participant, said it was difficult for him to hit the tennis ball hard into the fence—an exercise that I use for people to experience their raw power. After reflecting for a while on what was preventing him from simply letting it rip, Vince described how he had been brought up to please others, holding back his own wants and needs because serving others was considered more important.

Later, when we repeated the exercise on court, Vince played like a new person. After seeing and understanding his pattern, he was free to show us his power, and he enjoyed it, living his total energy.

Abby, a forty-five-year-old guy with a strongly competitive attitude, described a recent doubles match in which he considered himself to be the weakest player. He regarded this match as important. He knew the other players and felt nervous about meeting their standards of skill. He was unable to use his own racket because he had not expected to play. Instead, he had to borrow one from another player.

"I was horrified to be handed a racket that looked as if it had been made for kids. It was very small, and the strings seemed to have no life in them," Abby explained. "I looked at my partner and said, 'Well, I can't do anything with this, you're on your own.'

"When I accepted the fact that the racket was useless and I couldn't do anything, all my nervousness left me and I felt very relaxed. Then, to my surprise, I started to play good tennis. My strokes worked, my shots went in. We lost, but I felt I'd played as well as the other guys."

The experience of relaxation, the absence of goal orientation, both of which were normally difficult for Abby, had raised his game, allowing more of his potential to surface.

Staging Mock Contests

In another group sharing, two guys in their mid-thirties, Mike and Don, had just played a match against each other and felt it had not gone well.

I invited them to stand facing each other, ten feet apart, drew a line between them—like a net on a tennis court—then asked them to take their rackets and start making imaginary strokes. I asked them to keep looking at each other as they played, and to express how they were feeling with sounds or words. The other group participants sat in a circle around them, like an audience watching a match.

It felt a bit unnatural in the beginning, but with the encouragement of the group, Mike and Don started to get into it and express themselves. Mike began to play an aggressive, attacking game, saying things like, "Here, take this!" or "Now I've got you, you're dead!"

Don was more defensive, saying, "I'm still in this game. I don't give up so easily."

Their voices got louder, their breathing stronger, and it felt like a real fight.

When the exercise had reached a plateau, I asked them to stop, close their eyes, and feel what was going on inside.

In that silence, I could see that Don was deeply affected, and a tear slid out of the corner of one of his eyes. When I asked him to share what was going on, he said that he could see vivid pictures in his mind of when he was eight years old, playing football with his older brother, who was eleven. He recalled that, no matter how hard he tried, he could never win. His brother was too big, too fast, too strong.

Don went on to say that, while playing with Mike, he had felt unable to use his full energy, and he was convinced that he could not win. It became obvious to both Don and the group that his old feelings of helplessness were still shaping his way of playing as an adult. He was still carrying the wound from the experience with his brother.

I suggested that next time such feelings surfaced during a match he should allow them to be as conscious as possible, giving them space, while at the same time breathing deeply into his belly. He should stop playing, sit on the bench, close his eyes, and allow the feelings to be present, giving them space.

"For this, you need a safe environment; you need to be playing with someone who will understand what is happening and support your exploration," I told him.

Mike, when his turn came, said that although he had enjoyed being the dominant competitor, he didn't like the feeling that Don hadn't given him a real fight. "After a while, I felt like I was being mean, so I started to hold my energy back and I didn't enjoy it," he reported.

I explained to Mike that there is a difference between playing with totality and being aggressive toward your opponent. "You don't have to feel that you're crushing the other guy in order to play with your full power," I explained.

The process triggered by Mike and Don continued with everybody in the group engaging in mock tennis matches, then sharing their experiences with each other afterward. Such structures can provide deep insights into the way we live our lives, the attitudes we develop, and the past experiences that still affect us. Moreover, because the tennis is imaginary, these mock contests immediately take people beyond the level of discussing their strokes.

By the way, I would like to emphasize that not every realization or insight in a Zennis group sharing has to be of major psychological proportions. It can be something simple and straightforward, like Abby's understanding of the effect of relaxing while playing a match. There is no need to feel that you have to come up with some life-changing revelation each time it's your turn to share. Resist the temptation to become each other's psychoanalysts.

PLAYING

It's important to see how sharing relates to playing. It is the on-court playing time that provokes your inner reality, generating the feelings and attitudes about which you are later going to talk, so it is helpful for members of the Zennis support group to play regularly together.

Often it's quite difficult to get a bunch of players together, because of the time pressure of jobs, families, and other commitments, but it would be a good start if you can initiate a once-a-week session of about two hours of playing time. This can become a regular time and date at which group members know they can turn up and find people to play with.

There are basically two ways to meet and play: One is to explore the exercises that I have described in this book. The other is to play points in a competitive style. The competitive approach is more likely to bring up personal issues, and the practice sessions are likely to provide new experiences and a deeper quality of relaxation.

For balance, you can agree to experiment with exercises for one month, then play matches for the following month, and so on.

Team Tennis

With a small group of people and a relatively short period of playing time, it may seem that you can't do much, but in fact there are many variations with which you can experiment, particularly if you have two courts available instead of only one.

If you have four people, you can form two teams. If you have eight people, you can form four teams. You can create a small tournament, with four teams playing a combination of singles and doubles matches over a period of days or weeks.

In a four-team contest, Team A plays Team B with two singles matches and one doubles match, and the team that takes two out of the three matches has won. Meanwhile, Team C has been playing Team D. The winners of the two contests play each other, and so do the losers.

Tie-Breaker Scoring

You can greatly compress the time period for such tournaments if you play your matches as tie breakers. Professionals sometimes do this in exhibition matches, and it works well as an alternative form of competition. In a tie-breaker set, the player who is first to make seven points with a minimum difference of two points has won the set. For example, if you beat me 7–5, we have played 12 points and you have won the first set. To win a match, you need to win two tie breakers.

In this way, the longest match lasts only about fifteen minutes. Within forty-five minutes you can have two singles and one doubles match completed—that's the maximum time.

If you start with eight people in four teams, you can play the other team match within the same time frame, then the two winners play the final, while the two losers play for third and fourth place. Within two hours you can easily complete the tournament.

With this structure you don't get stuck with one person. The opponents keep changing, the energy keeps moving, and the mood of such contests is usually playful and fun.

Round-Robin

Another structure to explore is the round-robin. In this format, each player in your Zennis support group plays all of the other members, one at a time, making separate appointments for their matches according to their own schedules. This is a good structure if you can't manage to meet on a regular weekly basis.

It can be helpful to keep a diary so that if something significant happens in a match and your next group sharing session is a week or two away, you can write it up and share it later.

In a round-robin structure with a lot of individual matches it is a good idea to create at least one occasion per month when the whole group meets on court. In this way, the group energy stays dynamic and alive.

MEDITATING

I talked about meditation at some length in chapter 6 and suggested several effective meditation techniques that can be done either alone or with a group of people.

It is through meditation that you develop the art of looking within and becoming aware of your inner reality. You also become more detached, creating more space between you and the events you experience.

It is a good idea if group members can meditate regularly for a half hour a day. It is usually impractical to do this together, given the normal time constraints, but each member can do it alone. The best time for this is in the early morning around sunrise, but if this is too demanding on those who face a working day ahead, you can select another time that is more convenient.

Make it a point that when your support group meets you also meditate together, even if it is just for ten minutes of silent sitting at the beginning and end of the meeting. It may seem a little odd to get together and then do nothing, but meditation will change the quality of your time together.

CELEBRATING

A Zennis support group is a good excuse to live life more spontaneously and enthusiastically than you would by yourself. In a way, you're using sport as an opportunity to celebrate yourself. And sport is, after all, intended to be fun. The very word suggests an activity that is a lot less serious than either daily work or Sunday morning spirituality.

You don't need to wait until you've won a match or a tournament to celebrate. You can break this old pattern very easily, understanding that it is in the nature of competition for one person to win and the other to lose. If you have played with your totality, then even if you lost there will have been many moments when you were on top, many strokes that gave you satisfaction, many great points that you scored.

If you have won, you need to celebrate your opponent whose efforts allowed you to have this experience of victory. Without him, there would have been no match, no contest, no opportunity to test your skill.

In this way, the possibility arises that winning and losing will shed some of their stigma. Of course, the excitement and challenge of competition will remain, but there will be no question of feeling inferior as a person when you lose, or superior when you win.

It can be fun to schedule tennis-related events that are more like games than real matches. Here are a few that I have enjoyed with group participants.

In the Can

Pool your money and buy a few bottles of champagne. Place a large-sized garbage bin on the service line of the tennis court, halfway back from the net. The object of the game is to hit a ball into the can from the other side of the net. Each player pays for a chance, using six balls (this is one way to pay for the champagne) and has a choice: He can stand on the service line and try to hit a ball into the bin, being rewarded with a glass of champagne if he succeeds. Or he can try from the baseline, being rewarded with a whole bottle.

Left-Handed Tennis

Play a match of left-handed tennis. If you are already left-handed, play right-handed.

Monkey Tennis

This game is described in chapter 4, page 74.

Switching Hands

Play a match in which you play right-handed for one stroke and left-handed for the next.

Volleyball Tennis

Play a match rather like volleyball, in the sense that when the ball lands on your side of the net, you don't hit it back immediately, but you can touch it twice with your racket, allowing two bounces. This is especially fun in doubles, where you can pop it up for your partner to hit. It becomes a game of great skill and sensitivity when you don't play for winning points but to have as many rallies as possible with the other team.

Mini-Tennis

Play mini-tennis, using only the boxes in which the serves have to land. This brings the players closer together and breaks down the feeling of long-distance warfare created by a full-sized court. It can be very playful, requiring delicate and skillful shots.

Each One Teach One

Give each other tennis lessons. This is a great way to get to know each other and even if you are a relatively new player, you will be surprised how much you can contribute to your partner's understanding of his or her game.

Spend thirty minutes each, acting as a trainer for your partner on the court. Focus on some aspect of your partner's game that requires attention. You don't need to be an expert, offering technical advice that you picked up from reading the latest tennis magazine. Just be natural and authentic. You can ask very simple questions like:

"How did that stroke feel?"

"Were you happy with it?"

"Where in your body did you feel tense?"

You can make observations, such as, "You looked a little worried when you walked up to serve," or "It seems you are holding your breath when you make that stroke."

To be in the role of a trainer is itself a great training, because you need to be totally present, here and now, open and available, giving your undivided attention to the other person. These are, in fact, a coach's most important qualities.

The exercise also helps to break down the sense of hierarchy that "He is a better player than I am, so I have nothing to offer." Moreover, by helping your partner you're also helping yourself, working on your own game.

A FINAL WORD

Finally, a word about the overall purpose of your Zennis support group. Together, you are learning a totally new way of playing tennis—and also of living life—amid an overall climate of competition that emphasizes winning, comparison, the need for recognition, the glorification of fame, and success.

These are powerful pulls on the individual psyche, so don't be under any illusions about the atmosphere in which you are experimenting with Zennis. In addition, you will probably be playing in a club or a public facility where people play in the normal way, so you may feel a little uncomfortable at first.

However, if you are having fun together, feeling alive, juicy, then instead of being overwhelmed by the surrounding attitudes you may even find yourselves attracting new members. Zen is a playful and nonserious approach to life. If you and your friends are enjoying yourselves, happy to be together on an adventure of self-discovery, glad to be in the company of a few like-minded players on the path, that is enough to keep you on the right track.

With One Arrow

A hunter was chasing deer through the forest when he came upon a Zen master giving instruction to his disciples.

"How many deer can you kill with one arrow?" inquired the master.

"Why, one of course, and then only if I am lucky," replied the hunter.

"That is nothing," said the master. "With one arrow I can bring down the whole herd."

"What a terrible waste of life!" cried the hunter, dismayed at the idea.

"If you know this much, why don't you shoot yourself?" said the master.

At that moment the hunter realized that the master was not talking of hunting deer but of slaying the ignorance of humanity with the arrow of awareness. Presenting his bow to the master, the hunter said, "Since you have the arrow, why don't you shoot me?" and kneeling down, asked for initiation.

13
A New Vision for Competition

When I was a young man, I thought I was Superman. At sixteen, I was a promising tennis player, but the athletic arena in which I excelled was a team sport called handball.

I was really good at it, especially in goal-scoring. The most important thing in my life was to shoot ten goals every game, and since a handball match typically ends with a score of around 20–18, I would, on many occasions, shoot half the goals scored by our team. I'd throw ten and the next-best guy would probably make four.

I was still a junior but was quickly accepted in the adult team and within three months had become the best player. I pushed myself hard in the practice sessions, trying to jump higher, throw harder, and run faster than anybody else. I would not have admitted it at the time, but the motivation for this effort was to be the star, the Michael Jordan of our little handball team, based in a small village in the German countryside.

My school life had been mostly normal, a bit monotonous, and at a certain stage—around eleven years old—was filled with wounds of bullying, alienation, and a sense of being an outsider. My parents had just moved to the village, and I didn't seem to fit in with the other guys. Handball became the focus of my social life, a way to reach out and meet people.

I loved the recognition that I received, both from the other players and also from our supporters. I was the special guy, the local hero, and the greatest satisfaction was to hear how the other players talked about me: "You can count on Peter. He will always make his points."

I never paused to think about it, but for me winning a handball game was directly linked to winning people's appreciation and recognition. To be valued as a player allowed me to value myself.

I guess it's the same for most young people. At that age, when the hormones are bursting through your skin and you have more energy than you know what to do with, you are eager to find the challenges and the opportunities through which you can prove yourself in the eyes of others.

However, when you pause to think about it, this attitude begs some pretty fundamental questions, not only about the ambitions of young sports jocks, but about the value system that is unquestioningly embraced along with the games we play.

THE NEED FOR RECOGNITION

Why, in the first place, should we need public recognition in order to feel good about ourselves?

Isn't it a bit strange that our sense of self-worth should be dependent on other people's support and confirmation? And what if this support isn't forthcoming? Should we feel unworthy because others don't understand or appreciate us?

I'm not saying that it's a bad thing for young men and women to challenge themselves, test their strength, and enjoy competing against each other. I'm simply saying that to associate these activities with a craving for other people's approval seems unnecessary.

In my understanding, the need to look for validation outside ourselves has something to do with the way we are educated, the way we are taught from early childhood to estimate our value not in terms of personal individuality—just the way we are—but in terms of how well we perform, compared to others, in meeting the ideals and expectations of society.

This is an ancient and efficient survival strategy, developed by every kind of social group to ensure its continuing existence. It is based on the assumption that if the group is to survive, then the individual must be subordinated to the needs of the group.

For example, in our tribal past, the most useful and essential qualities required of a young man were hunting and fighting. Those who excelled in these talents, fulfilling the tribe's needs, were honored, and those who could not were despised.

When you think about it, nothing much has changed, especially in the area of sport. Those who bring home victory and glory to the tribe are the heroes. Nobody is interested in the losers. Just look at the sports pages of any newspaper and you will see what I mean.

When I started to look more deeply into my own motives

for excelling at sport, I could clearly see my hunger for recognition, and the lengths I went to get it. Of course, even without such motivation I would have been good at handball, since I had a natural talent for all kinds of ball games. I would still have enjoyed the energy, the excitement, the teamwork, the shooting, and the winning, but without that desperate, underlying need to be accepted and recognized that makes competition such a deadly serious affair for so many athletes.

MAKING THE RANKINGS

At nineteen, I felt a natural sense of completion with handball and began to focus exclusively on tennis, which offered an unexplored field of possibilities. For several years I was a self-taught player. I did not have a trainer but practiced mainly with a friend. Together we would study the successful players, learn through observation, then try out their techniques in practice and match play.

At twenty, I was giving lessons in a tennis school in Southern Germany when the owner, a former professional player, stopped me one day and said, "What are you doing here when you could be playing tournaments, making ATP points, and some money for yourself?"

I was surprised that anyone would consider me good enough to be listed in the world rankings, but then, almost immediately, it became a dream of mine to read my name on the printout of the world's top 500.

Next winter, together with my tennis buddy, Stefan, I flew to the West Coast to play a satellite circuit in Southern California: five tournaments in five weeks in five cities around Los Angeles. The competition was fierce, but it was a beautiful experience for me because I had to play twenty-eight matches in five weeks, and as a result my game improved dramatically.

I emerged from a qualifying field of 256 players to be selected for the master's tournament in Las Vegas, where I finished tenth. Being number ten meant that I had earned one ATP point, and the next week I was able to fulfill my ambition, reading my name on the world ranking list in the following manner:

No. 1 Bjorn Borg

No. 2 Jimmy Connors

. . . No. 500 Peter Spang (along with about fifty other players who also had one point)

In those days there were only ten German players who had ATP points, and I was proud of my achievement, but, to my surprise, I also felt a little flat. I had achieved my goal. Now what? I went back to Germany, not feeling particularly driven to climb higher in the ATP hierarchy, and for a couple of years I continued to play team tennis for a city club.

MEETING NIKI PILIC

Then I met Niki Pilic, the famous player and coach from former Yugoslavia. He showed interest in working with me, expressing his conviction that I had the potential to reach the top 100, even though I had started late. He further told me that, in his opinion, I was more talented than the German Davis Cup players whom he was coaching at the time.

Pilic's recognition of my talent fired me with new energy

and determination, and soon I was training and practicing like never before, rising swiftly in the world rankings from a lowly 500 to a promising 250. There were periods when I was constantly tired and exhausted, when I was clearly over-trained, as they call it nowadays, but the pace of my improvement kept me motivated.

After about six months I started to become aware of the price I was paying for my career. For one thing, I had entered a genuine love relationship for the first time in my life and did not willingly spend weeks and weeks on the professional circuit, living in hotel rooms, playing minor tournaments, when I knew I could be at home relaxing in the arms of a beautiful woman.

For another, the players with whom I traveled were mostly younger than me, ambitious seventeen- and eighteen-year-olds who were mad about tennis, undivided in their energy, hungry to win—rather like I had been as a young handball player. I couldn't find much in common with them. I was becoming interested in so many other things—vegetarianism, ecological issues, the politics behind sporting events—and there was no one with whom to share my ideas.

A player on tour needs some feeling of companionship in the long hours between matches and practice sessions. If this is absent, then professional tennis is a lonely life. This is not just my experience. It is the situation of many players, and it's something the public doesn't normally see or read about.

The media may be interested in a love affair between Thomas Muster and Fergie, Duchess of York, or in what Andre Agassi wore when he appeared with Brooke Shields at a party in Manhattan, but it is definitely not interested in the boredom and loneliness experienced by hundreds of young hopefuls as they hang around some dull city, awaiting their turn to play in a second- or third-class tournament.

Still, I persisted in my drive for self-improvement. I was playing well and with Pilic's guidance attained a new personal best by winning the Bavarian indoor championships.

TURNING POINT

Then something happened that cut right through my sense of priorities. Betsy, an old friend living in Ojai, California, called to say that she had been diagnosed with advanced cervical cancer and the doctors had told her that she was going to die.

From one moment to the next I decided to be with her. Within hours I was on a plane to the West Coast, and for the next few weeks I stayed in her house—no training, no practice, no matches—just talking with her or sitting silently while she slept or going for walks in the canyons.

It became a period of self-reflection for me, especially when I discovered a book in her library by the philosopher and mystic, J. Krishnamurti. The book was called simply *Life!* and although I cannot now remember what Krishnamurti was saying, it certainly kept the wheels of my mind spinning on a very different track from tennis, as did the proximity of death in the form of my friend's illness.

But the most powerful experience in Ojai was also the most unexpected. In the process of saying good-bye, Betsy showed me in a dozen different ways, through her eyes, her smile, her words, how happy she was that I had come to see her, that I had valued our friendship enough to drop everything in Europe and come to California.

Somehow in this meeting, in this simple dialogue between two friends, I felt deeply loved and respected, and quite obviously it had nothing to do with me winning tennis matches. I got it for free. I just had to be there, holding her hand. It was a deeply fulfilling experience, a profound realization that just how I am—without striving for any achievement—is more than enough.

In one of those fortunate flukes of fate, Betsy did not die, and when it seemed that her condition had stabilized, I returned to Europe. There, I encountered real problems trying to reenter the professional tennis scene. I was out of shape. I had to train vigorously just to regain my basic level of physical fitness, and Pilic believed in pushing people hard.

After a couple of weeks I had to ask myself, "Why am I torturing myself like this?" The answer was clear: for the rankings, for the chance to crack the top 100. It was also becoming difficult for me to accept Pilic's well-intentioned but aggressive approach to the game, the attitude that "If you want to be good, you gotta eat shit first."

My experience in Ojai had changed me. The drive for recognition did not have the same hold over me. I didn't need to beat other people just to feel good about myself, and I could see that if I put aside my ambition and tuned in to my real feelings, I was through with professional competition. It was time to quit.

Pilic and I remained friendly, and he told me later that he made a mistake in training me like "a worker" rather than as "an artist." To him, Germans are "workers" and they need to be driven hard, whereas he regarded me as "the only German player who is a Bohemian." But I don't honestly think it would have made much difference. I was more than ready to explore the world beyond tournament circuits.

A NEW APPROACH

At this delicate point, when a professional quits, there are really only two possibilities. He either hangs up his racket and drops the game completely—often with feelings of disappointment, bitterness or regret—or, if an authentic love for tennis remains, he finds a creative way to continue with the sport.

I chose the latter course and, as I explained earlier in the book, began a career in coaching. But it wasn't just a question of switching from player to coach. The change went deeper than that. My whole relationship to the game, my whole approach to sport, my whole attitude toward competition was undergoing a transformation. In particular, I wanted to find out which values, if any, could replace the motivations that had driven me since I was a teenager.

If there is no compelling need for a player to prove himself in the eyes of others, to seek recognition by beating another competitor, what remains? Is there a less primitive, more enjoyable way of competing?

Two conversations with Tim Gallwey, author of *The Inner Game of Tennis,* helped to shape a new perspective for me. I had read Gallwey's book and was determined to meet him, so when I stayed in Southern California for three months in 1987, living in Beverly Hills on an extended honeymoon with my wife, I obtained Gallwey's phone number and called him up. A few days later we met in his house in Malibu.

One of the first things we did was to spend an hour playing tennis on his private court. Ironically, even though I wanted to learn his approach, my competitive instincts rose up, and I was determined to beat both him and his method.

Since he was the older man and I was still in good shape, it wasn't difficult.

At the end, Gallwey laughed and said, "It's hard to practice what you preach when you face strong competition." I liked the easy way he accepted the situation. Then we started to talk.

Offering a model for a new sporting ethic, Gallwey spoke to me, as he does in his book, about the surfer who goes into the ocean to challenge the waves. Once a surfer develops a certain degree of skill, he doesn't take just any wave. He waits for the right wave, the wave that will produce the right level of challenge for his skill.

If we transfer this metaphor to the game of tennis, then facing the right opponent is like choosing the right wave. A good opponent is one who will challenge you to fulfill your potential. At the end of the match, you can thank him for the experience, regardless of whether you won or lost, because he provoked the best in you. Then shaking hands is a genuine act of gratitude, not the hollow gesture that you see so often on television.

Gallwey's metaphor of the surfer and the wave is helpful because it adds an element of cooperation to the naked battle of competition, but for me it was only a stepping-stone on my path of self-inquiry. The real answer to my quest came through the glimpses of meditation that I experienced first as a player, then as a coach, and later through meditation techniques.

THE ZEN PERSPECTIVE

Meditation led me to the Zen perspective on life, to the art of seeing the outer world as a reflection of my own inner reality.

In Zen, there is no competition. Of course, there is a tennis court, an opponent, a score, and a drama that is being enacted. But really it's only about you. It's about you and your consciousness, you and your life, you and your potential: how close you can get to the full expression of your creativity, your talent, your being.

You may be playing someone who is a better player than you or equal to you or worse than you. In a way, it doesn't matter. There is no need to wait for the right wave; and remember, in a tournament you can't choose your opposition. You can't decide who you play. You have to face whoever makes it through the previous round.

For the Zennis player, what really matters in any game—in any act of daily life, for that matter—is the internal experience. If you are happy with yourself, if you are centered, relaxed, alert, and fresh, then your play will reflect this state of inner harmony.

The Zen attitude may seem light-years away from the values of today's top professional players, but occasionally incidents happen that cast a totally different light on how the game can be played.

WIMBLEDON: A STANDING OVATION

For example, in the 1996 quarterfinals at Wimbledon, the African American, Malivai Washington, was playing a young German, Alexander Radulescu. It was a close match, building toward a thrilling climax with 6,000 people watching. The score was four to four in the fifth set with Washington serving, when the American hit a backhand volley on the line and the referee called the ball out, declaring, "Love–15." The chance for a break and victory for Radulescu were very close, with the semifinal and over $150,000 in prize money staring him in the face.

But Radulescu walked toward the referee and corrected the call, saying, "The ball was good." Spontaneously, the entire audience rose up and gave Radulescu a standing ovation that lasted several minutes. The gesture became one of the most talked-about incidents in the tournament, and much was said in the British media in praise of the German's sporting behavior and sense of fair play.

I take a different view of the incident. I'm convinced that when Radulescu corrected the referee's decision and gave the point to Washington, he was not thinking about fair play, good sportsmanship, or moral etiquette.

To me, it was the spontaneous response of someone who is already rich in himself, who does not need to steal points from the other guy out of a desire to win. Radulescu had, in a Zen sense, already won. He was already happy with himself. He was playing in the quarterfinals of the world's most important tennis event, and he was playing great tennis—by far the best in his young professional career.

Because it was Radulescu's first time in such a situation there was an innocence and beauty about him that tends to evaporate once a player becomes more established as a professional. When you reach the top ten, when it's expected that you will make the quarterfinals, when you know that the media will pan you if you don't put on a good show, then you can't afford to lose points by correcting bad calls given in your favor.

Then you are more of a businessman, a calculating competitor. Then you have to think of all kinds of consequences, such as the reaction of your sponsors: What are they going to say if you give away a crucial point, then lose the match, when you could have been wearing their logo on your shirt in the semifinal or even in the final? And you have to wonder whether, under such circumstances, they are going to renew your contract.

Washington was touched by Radulescu's gesture, commenting, "I have never experienced that a player in such a match, in such a tournament, would correct a point to his own disadvantage. I thank Alex for his fairness. I do not know if I would have done the same." Such a simple thing, a correction of a bad call, but the world of tennis has become so businesslike that it causes a sensation.

The audience gave Radulescu an ovation because they were touched, they were moved, they felt they were participating in something rare, something beautiful, something that loses its magic if you start to talk in terms of fair play and good sportsmanship.

FREE TO BE INDIVIDUALS

It has nothing to do with morality. Radulescu was simply being himself, and for me, this is the golden rule of Zennis: not that players should be good sports, but rather, that they should be themselves. They should feel free to be individuals, to be natural and authentic in the way they play the game. Then whatever they do is going to be entertaining, enthralling, touching.

One reason why audiences get bored with tennis these days is because of the conformity of behavior among the professionals. People complain, with good reason, that a few years ago there were more colorful characters on the pro scene: people like Connors, McEnroe, Navratilova, and Evert. Their complaints do not fall on deaf ears, because the sponsors, the managers, the people who control the game know they must keep their audiences entertained if they are to continue to profit from the tennis industry.

So they also start to wonder: Where are the characters? And they don't seem to realize that they themselves are responsible for the bland uniformity of the players. They are criticizing their own product, their own creation.

It comes down to education, how the young players get trained. Most people aren't aware of it, but the scouts are out there, searching for new talent even before the stage of junior tournaments, looking for the best of the ten- to twelve-year-olds, ready to offer contracts to those who show enough promise and potential. Immediately, the game has a business angle, a commercial dimension.

For example, Tommy Haas, whom Nick Bollettieri has described as "the most talented all-round player that I have coached in my thirty-nine years as a trainer," was sent to Bollettieri's tennis academy in Florida at the age of twelve and has lived and trained there for six years, far from his Bavarian home.

His father, a tennis teacher, financed his son's education by inviting 15 partners to each invest $35,000 over a period of five years. In return, they each receive one percent of Haas's earnings from pro tournaments.

His story is fairly typical. The kids with the most talent go to tennis schools where they eat the same, drink the same, play the same. Never mind finesse, go for power. Never mind working on your backhand, run around the ball and smash it with your forehand. Never mind if you're feeling shaky or inferior, keep acting like a winner.

Then you end up with fifty young players, all good athletes, all trained professionals, all conditioned to be mentally tough, all behaving the same way in the tournaments. You missed a shot? Never mind. Don't show anything. Follow the method: Turn away, look at your racket strings, walk back to the baseline, act as if you just won the point, think like a winner.

Nobody does anything unexpected, spontaneous, or human. Nobody breaks out of the pattern. And the chances are that the final will be slugged out between two baseline players hitting the ball in a mechanical, businesslike way, and that the next tournament will be a repetition of this one.

No wonder the audiences get bored at times. People want to be part of something real, and the realness is often missing. They want to feel inspired, and the inspiration is missing. They want to feel the heart, soul, and blood. That's why they loved Radulescu; because in that moment he did something that they would love to have done themselves.

True, a few top players, like Agassi, can put on a show. They can hold the racket to their head in a comic way, after a bad shot, as if wanting to shoot themselves for making such a stupid mistake. They can offer the racket to someone in the audience, as if to say, "Okay, you can probably play better than me right now." But when you have seen the same gestures a few times, you begin to suspect that it's not really spontaneous, just a bit of Las Vegas show biz.

A FRESH LOOK AT THE GAME

There is not much that I, as an individual, can do to create positive change in the international tennis world, but I would like to provoke tennis lovers to look at the game with fresh eyes. I would like to encourage them to develop their own opinions about which players are entertaining to watch, about which matches are worthwhile, not to merely follow the media, which in turn blindly follows the rankings.

I'd like people to start looking for those matches where players have some heart, some humor, some feeling, and where competitors hug each other at the end of a match, applaud each other for making good shots, and express themselves in an authentic and spontaneous way.

My vision for competition is that all top professional players should walk out onto the tennis court already feeling like winners, not in the sense of training themselves to be mentally tough, but because they are meditators, because they have explored their inner world and discovered the treasures that enable them to feel whole, complete, and in love with themselves and with life.

From this Zen space, they can play in a totally different way. The key words here are respect, love, and dignity, first for yourself, then, as a natural by-product, for other players. If international competition can become a stage where these qualities are displayed, then more spectators will come to these tournaments than the stadiums can hold, because people know they will leave feeling inspired and uplifted.

In addition, I would like players to handle postmatch interviews in a totally different way. Right now, the winner rushes from one TV interview to the next, all given in haste, all superficial in content, while the loser disappears into the crowd, not to be seen again until the next tournament.

I'd like both players to share much more of their inner processes. For example, as soon as the match has finished, the two competitors can sit down, close their eyes, and meditate for a couple of minutes, taking time to absorb what has happened. The audience can also participate.

Then one interviewer, representing all the TV networks,

can interview the two contestants for about five minutes, encouraging them to share their experiences—not just the forehands and backhands, but whatever psychological or spiritual insights they had during the match, whatever inner challenges they had to face.

I think this kind of interview would be especially helpful for very young players, who are the most easily influenced by TV role models. If they see champions talking freely about their doubts, fears, and weaknesses when facing competition, as well as their moments of courage, generosity, and triumph, this will encourage the kids to do the same. If they see only cool, superficial images, that's what they will absorb and imitate.

HONORING EVERY PLAYER

I'd also like to see a ceremony at the end of every Grand Slam tournament in which all the players are honored. After all, it is through the efforts of more than 120 competitors that the eventual champions are created. Without them, the winners are nothing. It would be appropriate, therefore, for all the players to assemble on center court and for the champions to present them with medals of participation, thanking them individually.

But the Zennis perspective extends far beyond the Grand Slams. It's not just a question of honoring professional players in a major tournament.

It's about creating a general climate in which every individual who picks up a tennis racket honors himself or herself, curious to see how the game can help them explore their individuality.

It's about encouraging tennis lovers to add the freshness

of meditation to their game, and for meditators to add the spice of tennis to their meditations.

Ultimately, it's about you—about the challenge of living each moment of your life in a vital, spontaneous, and enjoyable way.

Endnotes

If you have enjoyed reading this book and would like to be kept informed about Zennis programs and events in the United States and Europe, you can contact Peter Spang via the following addresses:

IN THE UNITED STATES:

Zen Sports
93 Oak Drive
Ojai, CA 93023

IN EUROPE:

Zen Sports
Kapuzinerstr. 25/1
D-80337 Munich
Germany

Music tapes and CDs to accompany Osho Dynamic Meditation and Osho Kundalini Meditation (described in chapter 6) can be obtained through the following music distribution companies:

IN THE UNITED STATES:

New Earth Records
P.O. Box 2368
Boulder, CO 80306
Tel: 1-800-570-4074

IN EUROPE:

Dharma Music GmbH
Lindenstr. 1
23948 Stellshagen
Germany
Tel: +49 38825 44300
Fax: +49 38825 44303

Additional information about Osho meditations can be obtained from:

Osho Commune International
17 Koregaon Park
Pune 411 001
India

Made in the USA
Lexington, KY
05 July 2011